T0328644

Cambridge Elements ≡

Elements in Political Economy
edited by
David Stasavage
New York University

ONE ROAD TO RICHES?

How state building and democratization affect
economic development

Haakon Gjerløw
*Peace Research Institute
Oslo*

Carl Henrik Knutsen
University of Oslo

Tore Wig
University of Oslo

Matthew Charles Wilson
*University of South
Carolina*

CAMBRIDGE
UNIVERSITY PRESS

CAMBRIDGE
UNIVERSITY PRESS

University Printing House, Cambridge CB2 8BS, United Kingdom

One Liberty Plaza, 20th Floor, New York, NY 10006, USA

477 Williamstown Road, Port Melbourne, VIC 3207, Australia

314–321, 3rd Floor, Plot 3, Splendor Forum, Jasola District Centre,
New Delhi – 110025, India

103 Penang Road, #05–06/07, Visioncrest Commercial, Singapore 238467

Cambridge University Press is part of the University of Cambridge.
It furthers the University's mission by disseminating knowledge in the pursuit of
education, learning, and research at the highest international levels of excellence.

www.cambridge.org
Information on this title: www.cambridge.org/9781009054553
DOI: 10.1017/9781009053693

First published 2021

A catalogue record for this publication is available from the British Library.

ISBN 978-1-009-05455-3 Paperback
ISSN 2398-4031 (online)
ISSN 2514-3816 (print)

One Road to Riches?
How State Building and Democratization Affect Economic Development

Elements in Political Economy

DOI: 10.1017/9781009053693
First published online: November 2021

Haakon Gjerløw
Peace Research Institute Oslo

Carl Henrik Knutsen
University of Oslo

Tore Wig
University of Oslo

Matthew Charles Wilson
University of South Carolina

Author for correspondence: Haakon Gjerløw, haagje@prio.org

Abstract: Building effective state institutions before introducing democracy is widely presumed to improve different development outcomes. Conversely, proponents of this "stateness-first" argument anticipate that democratization before state building yields poor development outcomes. In this Element, we discuss several strong assumptions that (different versions of) this argument rests upon and critically evaluate the existing evidence base. In extension, we specify various observable implications. We then subject the stateness-first argument to multiple tests, focusing on economic growth as an outcome. First, we conduct historical case studies of two countries with different institutional sequencing histories, Denmark and Greece, and assess the stateness-first argument (e.g., by using a synthetic control approach). Thereafter, we draw on an extensive global sample of about 180 countries measured across 1789–2019 and leverage panel regressions, preparametric matching, and sequence analysis to test a number of observable implications. Overall, we find little evidence to support the stateness-first argument.

Keywords: state building, state capacity, democratization, economic growth, development

ISBNs: 9781009054553 (PB), 9781009053693 (OC)
ISSNs: 2398-4031 (online), 2514-3816 (print)

This Element has an appendix, which can be found online at
www.cambridge.org/OneRoadToRichesAppendix

Contents

1 Introduction

The history of global economic and political development is often told as a story of divergence. Some countries, such as Denmark and Switzerland, have followed favorable development paths over the last couple of centuries, and are today prosperous and peaceful democracies with strong state institutions. Other countries, such as Iraq and Ethiopia, have followed very different trajectories and are currently poorer, less peaceful, less democratic, and display weaker state capacity than Denmark or Switzerland. This "great divergence" has inspired a long scholarly debate about *how and why* some countries got to "Denmark" – Francis Fukuyama's (2004) metaphor for a society resembling the actual Denmark of present. Why is it that only some countries have followed a trajectory of state building, political liberalization, and economic growth that eventually resulted in societies characterized by good governance, democracy, and prosperity?

One prominent argument in this long-standing debate proposes that there is only one (or a handful) of development paths that actually lead to "Denmark." Crucially, particular institutions need to be introduced in a specific sequence; the road to "Denmark" involves adopting some features *before* others. We refer to such arguments – which come in different versions – as "sequencing explanations" of development. These explanations are thus not only concerned with the *configuration* of specific institutions (e.g., the existence and characteristics of free elections, independent courts, etc.) but of the timing and *historical sequence* in which institutions are adopted.

Perhaps the most widely regarded such "sequencing explanation" of development holds that building effective state institutions before introducing democracy has beneficial effects on numerous outcomes (see, e.g., Andersen and Doucette, 2020; Berman, 2019; D'Arcy and Nistotskaya, 2017; Fukuyama, 2007, 2014a; Mansfield and Snyder, 1995, 2007; Shefter, 1993; Zakaria, 2003). We refer to such explanations as "stateness-first" arguments, and in this Element we set out to critically discuss and empirically evaluate their validity. According to this view, the state-before-democracy pathway leads to "Denmark." Conversely, introducing democratic institutions, including competitive elections and universal suffrage, before effective and capable state institutions is a path to political instability, democratic backsliding, clientelism, or slow economic growth. In this Element, we focus on the latter outcome and examine whether building state capacity before introducing democracy really enhances economic growth when compared to institutional sequences where democracy is introduced before high state capacity is achieved. To preview our main finding, we find little support in the data for the notion that sequences of institutional adoption matter for economic growth.

The stakes in the debate over institutional sequencing and development outcomes are high. Identifying a correct answer to the question of how countries become stable, well-governed and wealthy is of immense importance to different types of policy prescriptions and diagnoses made by donors, governments, and other policymakers with an interest in promoting development. More generally, the sequencing debate has implications for when different reforms to state institutions, multi-party elections, and democracy-relevant civil liberties of various kinds should be introduced. If the stateness-first argument is correct, countries would be ill advised to pursue democratizing reforms before a capable state apparatus, staffed by meritocratically recruited and rule-following bureaucrats, is in place. But, if the stateness-first argument is wrong, yet governments believe it, we risk trading off democracy (now) for fictitious economic and other gains in the future.

Coming up with definite answers (or prescriptions), for each and every country, as to what role the sequencing of democracy and state building has played (or will play) in ensuring development is hard. Still, we can leverage what information we have available for looking at general patterns in the data. If the stateness-first argument is true, we should observe that countries that build state institutions before democratization – everything else equal – have higher rates of economic growth, for example. This is the type of assessment that we venture into in this Element.

1.1 The State of the Evidence

Stateness-first arguments have historically been, and still are, very popular among academics and policy makers. As Mazzuca and Munck (2014) note, the view that "to ensure successful democratization and enduring democracy, various challenges concerning the construction of a state must be tackled before the democracy question" is "widely treated as the conventional wisdom" (p. 1222). Variants of this position maintain that establishing certain institutions before democracy is favorable for development outcomes. Huntington (1968) argued that it is vital to ensure "political order" before introducing mass politics. Other influential early arguments suggest that nation building or state-institution building prior to the expansion of mass politics are important (Dahl, 1971; Rustow, 1970). An influential recent formulation of the stateness-first argument is found in Fukuyama's *The Origins of Political Order*. Like Huntington, Fukuyama focuses on expansions of the franchise to broad segments of the population and the initiation of "mass politics" when considering the process of democratization, arguing that those "countries in which democracy preceded modern state-building have had much greater problems achieving high-quality governance" (Fukuyama, 2014a, p. 30).

Despite its prominence, the evidence base supporting the stateness-first argument remains surprisingly limited, especially when it comes to large-N studies considering a variety of contexts. Fukuyama's (2004) empirical exploration, for example, is done in the vein of macro-historical sociology; inferences are drawn from (implicit and explicit) comparisons of specific historical trajectories, and the rules for case selection or how to measure key variables are unclear. This empirical approach is common also more generally in studies proposing stateness-first arguments. While this approach is narratively rich and nuanced, allowing scholars to trace finer-grained sequences of institutional adoption and other events, it also has its drawbacks. Notably, it lacks much of the rigor that is possible to achieve by employing statistical analysis of large-N data, making it hard to evaluate the evidentiary status of the argument. It is hard to determine, for example, whether state-first sequences *by necessity*, *often*, or *only in historically "important" cases* lead to, say, economic growth based on the approach followed by Fukuyama (and others). It is also hard to gauge the size of the purported effect and to tease the effect of stateness-first sequences apart from that attributable to correlated historical developments, such as industrialization, European imperialism, or institutional diffusion between neighboring countries.

1.2 Our Contributions

This Element takes a second look at the proposed superiority of the stateness-first path. We examine the relationship between stateness-first sequences of institutional adoption – when countries build up capable state institutions before democratizing – and economic development. We make two main contributions to this important debate. The first is theoretical; we clarify the stateness-first argument and try to specify a more rigorous and coherent version than what is often presented in extant accounts. We do so by specifying and evaluating critical assumptions and counterarguments and by elaborating on observable implications following from the argument. While our empirical tests focus on income levels and growth, our theoretical discussion also pertains to related outcomes coming after the sequence of institutional adoption but prior to growth in the causal chain, including corruption, clientelism, and the functioning and stability of democracy itself.[1]

---

[1] Sen (1999), for example, elaborates on how "development" is broader than only GDP per capita growth. Over the last few decades, many policy makers and academics have thus considered

Our second contribution is empirical. We systematically probe different expectations following from the stateness-first argument, focusing on income level and growth as outcomes. We use data from Varieties of Democracy (V-Dem), version 10 (Coppedge et al., 2020c), including new Historical V-Dem data (Knutsen et al., 2019), which extends relevant V-Dem indicators back to 1789. These extensive time series allow us to track institutional developments throughout modern history, covering important periods of state building and democratization across world regions.

To assess different assumptions and implications of the argument, we take a multi-pronged approach to testing. We first conduct historical case studies of one stateness-first case (Denmark) and one democracy-first case (Greece) and also analyze the role of institutional sequencing in these countries' development through a synthetic control approach. This approach involves constructing hypothetical counterfactual cases to, respectively, Denmark and Greece, by drawing on information from countries that experienced a different institutional sequencing history but that were otherwise similar in relevant regards. Thereafter, we turn to an extensive global sample of more than 180 countries, measured across 1789–2019, and leverage panel regressions to estimate how state capacity and democracy interact in affecting development. Next, we conduct pre-parametric matching to test different empirical implications of the stateness-first argument. With these analyses, we compare, for instance, (otherwise similar) high- and low-state capacity countries that underwent democratization episodes. Finally, we employ sequence analysis to test a core implication of the stateness-first arugment. For this analysis, we classify historical patterns of institutional adoption and use these classifications to investigate how different institutional sequences predict growth. Overall, we find little evidence to support the stateness-first argument.

Our empirical analyses also makes a methodological contribution to the literature on institutional sequencing and development, especially with our final analysis that maps historical institutional sequences. Here, we employ the relatively novel (to political science) methodology of sequence analysis (Casper and Wilson, 2015) to probe whether certain trajectories of institutional adoption – such as building states before democratizing, or vice versa – have benevolent

---

other aspects or measures of economic or human development, including health and education measures, measures considering the distribution of income or goods, or more direct measures of subjective well-being. Nonetheless, GDP per capita remains an integral part of economic development – capturing both average income and average production in a society – and is highly correlated with other development aspects such as education levels or infant mortality. There are also more pragmatic reasons for focusing on GDP measures rather than, say, subjective well-being or education measures; GDP data cover most countries of the world and have extensive time series, allowing for comprehensive cross-national tests.

effects on economic development. Sequence analyses add to more conventional panel data specification by enabling us to incorporate sequences (here, of institutional adoption) into empirical models. We are also, to our knowledge, the first to use synthetic control methods in this long-standing debate. Comparative case studies abound in the literature, and the synthetic control approach resembles this approach but provides additional rigor. Oftentimes, the compared countries differ on several relevant factors, making it hard to attribute differences in development to institutional sequences rather than alternate factors; a synthetic control approach allow us to construct better (though hypothetical) contrast cases.

That being said, we readily acknowledge the difficulties of drawing strong causal inferences on the basis of the results presented here. Indeed, the very nature of the question of how long-term development outcomes are affected by institutional sequencing greatly constrains the type of data and designs available for obtaining empirically informed answers. However, we consider the panel and cross-section evidence presented in this Element to represent clear improvements over much of the extant evidence. The analyses performed herein are grounded in more precise formulations of the stateness-first argument, and our data and specifications allow for more stringent testing of the (various) hypotheses flowing from the stateness-first argument than has hitherto been conducted.

1.3 Roadmap of the Element

In Section 2, we first briefly review evidence from the vast literature on how democracy affects economic growth, before we turn to the literature on state capacity and growth. Thereafter, we review the literature dealing with different sequencing theories of development, focusing in particular on the stateness-first argument. Finally, we flesh out a more specific version of the stateness-first argument and clarify the different links in the proposed causal chain from sequences of institutional adoption to economic growth.

In Section 3, we critically discuss the stateness-first argument's core assumptions and introduce and assess plausible counterarguments and evidence bearing on these assumptions. Next, we elaborate on various empirical implications from (different interpretations) of the stateness-first argument and lay the groundwork for our empirical analysis by discussing how these different implications might be tested.

In Section 4, we discuss how to measure stateness-first sequences in a systematic manner across countries and over time. Crucially, we revisit the concepts of "democracy" and "capable state bureaucracy" and delve into how they can be – and are – measured using new data sources. We discuss how we follow previous stateness-first arguments in conceptualizing democracy as "electoral democracy," with a focus on contested elections and extensive suffrage. Further, we detail how we view state capacity as linked to the ability of state institutions to effectively implement government policies (in different policy areas), and how different "Weberian features" of the state bureaucracy are prerequisites for high state capacity. Next, we elaborate on our main operationalizations of these concepts, which rely on indicators and indices from the V-Dem dataset, and discuss different validity and reliability issues. We also present other operationalizations of our main concepts from different datasets. Finally, we discuss how we can go about operationalizing different institutional sequences that countries have followed historically, elaborating on and illustrating, for example, stateness-first as well as democracy-fist sequences. We also provide descriptive evidence of how common different sequences have been in different regions of the world throughout modern history.

In Section 5, we present two qualitative-historical case studies of Greece and Denmark. These two countries are considered as prime examples of, respectively, the "democracy-first" and "stateness-first" institutional sequences. We delve into these countries' histories of institutional development and how their sequences of institutional adoption may have influenced development trajectories. We thereafter present more systematic evidence on how these institutional sequences affected economic growth in both the Greek and Danish cases by using synthetic control methods.

In Section 6, we present our main analyses, conducted on more than 180 countries and with time series from 1789 to 2019. We present results from, respectively, panel regressions, matching analyses, and sequence analyses, testing different assumptions as well as implications from the stateness-first argument. In sum, we find little systematic evidence in support of the stateness-first argument.

In the concluding Section 7, we discuss how our findings can inform – or at least temper – prescriptive policy advice on the (un)desirability of promoting democracy in countries with weak state institutions. We also highlight avenues for future research, emphasizing that similar, careful studies are needed to assess whether stateness-first sequences have different effects on alternative outcomes such as regime stability, democratic quality, civil war, and human development.

2 Institutions, Development and Sequencing Arguments

Country rankings for important economic and political development outcomes, including democracy, bureaucratic quality, and income level, often identify similar sets of countries as high and low achievers. Why have some countries, such as Denmark, followed favorable development trajectories, both politically and economically, whereas others have not? One explanation is that political institutions influence economic development outcomes (Acemoglu et al., 2001; Acemoglu and Robinson, 2012; North, 1990; Rodrik et al., 2004). Despite the prominence of this "institutionalist view," there is no real consensus on exactly *which* institutions matter for spurring development. Two key suggestions are democracy and state capacity. In the following, we will briefly review the two related strands of literature, which tend to isolate the effect of either democracy or state capacity, without considering interactions between them. We then turn to discussing institutional sequencing arguments, where we put special emphasis on the stateness-first argument. But, first, we highlight two caveats pertaining to the stateness-first argument, in particular, and to institutionalist explanations of development, more generally.

First, there may be other "deep determinants" than institutions that affect economic development, and these determinants may simultaneously shape institutional development. Thus, it is hard to disentangle the effects of particular institutions, or sequences of institutional adoption, on development, and we should account for several alternative explanations in our empirical specifications. Of particular note are those explanations that describe how dynamics surrounding resource extraction shape state development, and that highlight the interrelation of coercion, resource extraction, and economic growth. A critical feature of successful state building is the state's ability to monopolize resources; states that are more reliant on extracting revenue from citizens – for example due to absence of natural resources or presence of an external security threat – will invest in developing the infrastructural capacity to induce compliance (Levi, 1989) and will make concessions and forge contracts with the owners of capital to legitimate tax collection (Tilly, 1990). Moreover, a high income level eases the funding of different investments in state capacity and incentivizes rulers to allocate resources to state building (see Besley and Persson, 2011). Hence, we should not only account for, for example, (country-specific) security threat environments when investigating how state capacity relates to economic growth, but also for initial levels of economic development.

Second, links between institutions, or sequences of institutional adoption, and economic development may be moderated by other factors. In this Element, we do not investigate all such sources of potential heterogeneity, leaving open the possibility that stateness-first sequences may have different implications for growth in different contexts. One notable type of explanation for differences in development trajectories concerns social groups and movements and, especially, the strength of organized labor (Mudge and Chen, 2014). Arguments about variation in state provision of welfare benefits hold that the balance of power between classes, and the coalitions that they form, shape the type and amount of concessions that citizens are able to secure from the government, and thereby the contents of economic policies. The power balance between classes also affects the institutionalization of class preferences in the form of political parties (Esping-Andersen, 1990; Kemeny, 1995). A strong state (that is able to implement whatever policy is passed in an efficient manner) may thus have very different implications for both economic development and democracy in societies dominated by different social groups. With these caveats in mind, we start our review of relevant institutionalist explanations of development.

2.1 Democracy and Economic Development

The literature linking democracy to development is vast. Reviews of this literature include Przeworski and Limongi (1993) and Knutsen (2012). In addition, Doucouliagos and Ulubaşoğlu (2008) and Colagrossi et al. (2020) provide meta-studies comprising several hundreds of estimates from cross-country regressions on economic growth. Here, we only give a brief overview of the most important theoretical arguments and findings.

As Przeworski and Limongi (1993) make clear, the sign of the aggregate relationship between democracy and growth is theoretically indeterminate; some mechanisms suggest that democracy enhances growth, whereas others suggest that democracy reduces growth. Theoretical arguments predicting that democracy mitigates growth have often focused on how democracy generates policies that reduce incentives for the accumulation of physical capital investment. The gist of the argument is that democracy could reduce growth because of pressures for immediate (public and private) consumption generated by short-sighted voters (Galenson, 1959; Schweinitz Jr., 1959). Due to contested elections, democratic leaders are presumably less autonomous from the preferences of the wider populace, which is supposedly less concerned about future growth than with satisfying immediate demands for consumption. In autocracies, where capital owners and other economic elites often govern, extensive public consumption can be sacrificed at the altar of increasing savings rates. This leaves more resources for investments in machinery, buildings, and other infrastructure, which enhance future growth (at least in the medium term). A related argument is that autocracies, due to fewer constraints on the executive, can more easily and speedily drive through economic reforms that are contentious, as certain groups in the economy lose out, but nonetheless yield long-term benefits for aggregate economic production. In democracies, interest groups may more easily act as veto players (Olson, 1982), whereas more autonomous autocrats can override them and pursue developmentalist policies (Przeworski and Limongi, 1993).

At the same time, several established arguments point to potential growth benefits of democracy. One argument centers on protection of property rights, which is widely held to mitigate investment uncertainty and thereby enhance several types of investments and innovation activities, and thereby growth (see, e.g., North, 1990; Romer, 1990). Democracy provides several checks against expropriation of property – such as a framework for guaranteeing civil liberties and ensuring rule of law – by the incumbent regime and its supporters. Unconstrained autocratic regime elites often engage in expropriation to fatten their own pockets or pay off crucial support groups (Acemoglu et al., 2001; Bueno de Mesquita et al., 2003; Knutsen, 2011a; Albertus and Menaldo, 2012; Ansell and Samuels, 2014). Insofar as democracy ensures more stable and broad-based property rights protection for all citizens, it should enhance growth. More generally, democracies placing constraints on the arbitrary (and predatory) interventions of rulers should lead to a more favorable business climate (e.g., Acemoglu and Robinson, 2012).

A second argument emphasizes the differing incentives of democratic and autocratic leaders to pursue educational and health policies. Since democracies are more responsive to citizens' preferences, including those of rural voters who typically have little political clout in autocracies, democracy increases growth relative to autocracy by providing widely demanded policies that enhance the human capital of the country. Such policies include expansion of primary and secondary school enrollment and spending on basic healthcare programs and facilities throughout the country (Lake and Baum, 2001; Lindert, 2005; Stasavage, 2005).

A third argument holds that democracy, by ensuring the protection of free speech, free media, free movement, and free assembly, enhances technological change. By protecting civil liberties, and thereby aiding the free flow of innovation and critical exchanges of ideas and learning in both the marketplace and the public sector, democracy may not only spur innovation but also the adaptation of new and efficient ideas and technologies generated abroad (e.g., Przeworski et al., 2000; Halperin et al., 2005; North, 2005; Knutsen, 2015). Since technological change is widely considered the prime determinant of long-term growth (e.g., Barro and Sala-i Martin, 2004; Acemoglu, 2008), this argument predicts a substantial development advantage of democracy relative to autocracy.

Turning to the empirical evidence on the aggregate relationship between democracy and growth, the results are somewhat mixed but, overall, point in favor of a positive effect of democracy on growth. Many early studies indicated a negative relationship (Przeworski et al., 2000; Doucouliagos and Ulubaşoğlu, 2008; Knutsen, 2012). However, more recent studies, which enjoy better data quality, longer time series, and more sophisticated model techniques to deal with reverse causality and unobserved, country-specific confounders, find positive and quite substantial effects of democracy on growth (e.g., Gerring et al., 2005; Knutsen, 2011b; Acemoglu et al., 2019; Colagrossi et al., 2020). Even these studies may underestimate the growth benefits of democracy. Missing GDP data is more common for autocracies than democracies and especially low-performing autocratic economies have more missing data (e.g., Halperin et al., 2005, 33). Also when data are reported, politicized statistical agencies and pressures for artificially inflating GDP numbers seem prevalent in autocracies (e.g., Magee and Doces, 2015). Nevertheless, there is sufficient variation in results to warrant caution on strong claims about the direction and strength of the relationship between democracy and growth.

2.2 State Capacity and Economic Development

Another literature has pointed to the relevance of the bureaucracy and the capacity of state institutions for economic growth. The arguments linking state capacity to growth are manifold, especially those predicting a clear, positive effect of state capacity. Several case studies – notably on high-capacity East Asian countries and low-capacity sub-Saharan African ones – have appealed to a competent bureaucracy as a key factor in explaining countries' development paths. One argument for why state capacity – and its core precondition, a bureaucracy with "Weberian features" (see Section 4) – should matter for growth, points to the role of effective implementation of policies for generating the intended consequences of economic policies, be it enhancing educational outcomes in the realm of schooling policies or enhancing capital investments in the realm of investment and industrial policies. A well-organized, rule-following, and autonomous bureaucracy staffed by meritocratically recruited, competent personnel should be better at adapting and implementing complex economic policies. Such bureaucracies may simultaneously be capable of extracting information from communities (to ensure that policies are appropriately designed for the local context) and be autonomous enough to resist pressures from antagonistic local groups who aim to derail effective implementation (Evans, 1995).

Second, an impartial and rule-following bureaucracy should enhance growth by upholding the rule of law and equal treatment under the law in matters pertaining to property rights protection and contract enforcement (see Cornell et al., 2020). Uncorrupt and rule-following bureaucrats should be less likely to favor businesses or other economic agents for personal reasons or be tempted to undermine the investments and other economic activities for their own (or political leaders') personal gain (North, 1990). Insofar as property rights enhance growth, a Weberian bureaucracy should contribute to higher growth via this channel. Another argument centers on the competence of bureaucrats. In states where bureaucrats are selected on their merits rather than personal ties and family bonds, the bureaucratic apparatus will work more efficiently and ultimately provide better public services in crucial sectors such as education, policing, and health care. This competence dividend should, in turn, increase growth. Furthermore, an administration that is rule-following, impartial, and which uses merit-based promotion makes patronage and clientelism less likely, which, in turn, reduces various inefficiencies in the allocation of productive resources (e.g., Fukuyama, 2014a). The norms encouraged by a rule-following bureaucracy can also reduce shirking and thus incentivize high-productivity behavior. Finally, state capacity also corresponds with states' ability to effectively penetrate, monitor, and coordinate activities that directly affect production and growth, such as the development of tax systems and key infrastructure (e.g., Brautigam et al., 2008).

Cornell et al. (2020) highlight several caveats, and even counterarguments, to some of the proposed mechanisms mentioned here. For example, discussing case studies of historical development and state involvement in the economy, Cornell et al. surmise that state capacity may have been less important for generating economic growth in the nineteenth century than at present, given the smaller role played by states in nineteenth-century economies and less complex production technologies (yielding less need for a competent bureaucracy to monitor and regulate private sector production). For similar reasons, Cornell et al. propose that a Weberian bureaucracy may be less important for generating growth in initially less developed economies, with less complex production technologies and a smaller public sector, than in developed economies.

It is also unclear why politicians in high-capacity states would have incentives to pursue economic policies with the aim of creating high growth, rather than some other objective:

> organizations with rule-following and competent staffers, Weberian bureaucracies can, in principle, implement any policy impartially and effectively. Indeed, if politicians, for some reason, decide to pursue monetary, fiscal, or industrial policies that mitigate growth, having a Weberian bureaucracy may exacerbate the negative effect of the policy, due to its effective implementation. This possibility extends beyond theory. Historical examples of countries pursuing growth-retarding policies abound, either because politicians

have legislated from misguided beliefs about what causes development, or because incumbents have had strong incentives to pursue particular economic policies despite knowing that they retard development. (Cornell et al., 2020, pp. 2252–2253)

As for the relationship between democracy and growth, the empirical evidence on state capacity enhancing growth is ambiguous. Many early studies relied on cross-section regressions, which are associated with several methodological issues such as picking up reverse effects from development on state capacity (see Cornell et al., 2020). Recent studies have used measures and designs that are less vulnerable to such reverse causality biases but the results have been mixed (Bockstette et al., 2002; Borcan et al., 2018; Cornell et al., 2020). Both historical case studies (e.g., on early versus late industrializers) and statistical analysis considering the potential non-linear and context-dependent nature of the relationship do, however, indicate that enhancing state capacity may be more important for growth in some situations than in others.

2.3 Sequences of Democracy and State Capacity and Various Outcomes: A Review of the Literature and Specifying the Arguments

In contrast to focusing on bivariate relationships between state building, democracy, and economic development, sequencing explanations consider how the *order* in which two of these variables develop affects the third. Different sequencing arguments figure prominently in the historical-comparative literature on development. While several scholars have rejected notions of institutional sequencing, questioning the factual basis of the proposed risks of "premature elections" or other specific "out-of-sequence" changes (Berman, 2007; Carothers, 2007; Hobson, 2012), sequencing arguments remain popular among scholars and in policy circles. Although this literature often frames the question in terms of "development" more broadly, sequencing arguments vary in whether they emphasize political institutions (democracy, stable government, etc.) or economic development as outcomes of interest.

Sequencing explanations of successful democratization, for example, propose that certain institutional (and other) preconditions need to be in place prior to the establishment of democracy. For example, Dahl (1971) argues that institutionalizing contestation among elites prior to expanding participation rights constituted the most stable pathway to democracy.[2] Huntington (1968),

---

[2] A related notion is that where state formation and democratization developed over *a protracted period of time*, they involved the rationalization of authority and establishment of control prior

to take another prominent example, argued "political order" is a requisite for economic development, which, in turn, opens up for successful transitions to democracy. Under what Fukuyama (2011) termed "authoritarian moderniza-tion," the state should first establish a modicum of stability and subsequently encourage economic development. Although growth and modernization did not depend directly on the strength of institutions, Huntington argued that strong institutions were necessary to constrain the destabilizing forces that economic development – and related social mobilization – unleashed. Following industri-alization and the emergence of a middle class supporting democratic practices and norms, democratization could then take root and succeed. Thus, accord-ing to Huntington, successful states were those in which the leader initially suppressed popular dissent and imposed state authority to construct institu-tions regulating competition and enforce laws. Insofar as political order partly results from professionalized and centralized bureaucracies, this suggests that one particular sequence involving state building, economic development, and democratization enhances long-term outcomes such as quality and stability of democracy.

Furthermore, the sequence in which particular democratic institutions are adopted may also influence long-term development outcomes. One variant of the argument focuses on the need for establishing "liberal" institutional features early on, with civil liberties prior to suffrage expansion being a con-dition for democratic deepening (Marshall, 1949; Zakaria, 2003; Møller and Skaaning, 2013). Such sequencing explanations often rely on a causal mech-anism where periods of learning are crucial. For example, Marshall (1949) emphasises that the British population enjoyed civil rights prior to political rights. The workers, he argues, learned how to utilize these rights and orga-nize into labor unions and eventually political parties. With time, they used their new-founded organizations to demand political rights and, in turn, social rights, creating the welfare state. More recently, Ziblatt (2017) argues that the most successful European democracies experienced a slow, step-wise intro-duction of democratic principles. By giving the elites time to learn how to compete in elections – that is, by organizing conservative parties and devel-oping campaign machines – these elites became less opposed to democracy. In countries where the conservatives did *not* have the time to learn the rules of the game, Ziblatt argues, they advanced tactics of electoral fraud to safeguard

---

to extending widespread participation rights in elections (Fukuyama, 2011, 2014a). More gen-erally, several sequencing arguments (e.g., Mansfield and Snyder, 2007) invoke the distinct notion of pace of democratization and state-building processes as important for outcomes, in addition to sequencing.

their interests (and fortunes) from the popular vote, to the detriment of democracy.

The stateness-first argument is one especially prominent type of sequencing argument, and its popularity extends back several decades. Following decolonization processes in Africa and Asia after WWII, several young democracies experienced newly elected leaders abusing their powers or competing interests degenerating into armed conflicts. These observations, we believe, helped spur scholars to theorize that the successful implementation of democracy, and subsequent effects on societal and economic developments, depends on its timing relative to state building. While other arguments suggest that "democracy-first" sequences may be beneficial for various outcomes (Stasavage, 2020) – for instance, because democracy helps countries resolve initial conflicts over redistribution or select accountable leaders, which are conducive to state building (Migdal, 1988; Scott, 1998) – "stateness-first" arguments remain popular among social scientists studying comparative development. Also more recently, several scholars have suggested that "postponed transitions" to democracy, and especially after rule of law or a high-capacity bureaucracy has been achieved, make countries less likely to experience violence, widespread patronage, or other bad economic policies and outcomes associated with a rushed transition (Shefter, 1993; Mansfield and Snyder, 2005, 2007; D'Arcy and Nistotskaya, 2017).

To focus the discussion, we provide a somewhat more detailed discussion of the recently formulated stateness-first argument in Fukuyama (2012, 2014a). Fukuyama's work presents an explicit sequencing argument that has become prominent. Further, Fukuyama's very plausible narrative is backed up by a number of case histories. Equally relevant for our purposes, it also seems belabored by several of the more general issues with stateness-first arguments that we discuss in Section 3.

Fukuyama (2012, 2014a) maintains that a strong state – defined by high *state capacity* and *rule of law* – is necessary for democratic longevity and economic success. Echoing Shefter (1993), Fukuyama (2014b) outlines the argument: "when a modern, Weberian state has coalesced prior to the expansion of the democratic franchise, it tends to resist colonization by patronage-dispensing politicians because it develops around it a protective 'absolutist coalition'" (p. 1333). Fukuyama invokes the concepts of patronage – the reciprocal exchange of favors between two individuals of different status and power – and clientelism – patronage on a larger scale – and treats clientelism as a consequence of unfettered democracy. This link is premised on democratic politics requiring the mass mobilization of voters (Fukuyama, 2014a, p. 86). If democracy is introduced *before* safeguards against clientelism – such as

Figure 1 The causal chain linking sequencing of institutions to economic growth.

merit-based recruitment to and impartial and rule-following behavior by the bureaucracy – democratic leaders will offer government positions for support. "Clientelism emerges in young democracies because the state and its resources constitute useful piggy banks for democratic politicians seeking to mobilize supporters" (Fukuyama, 2014a, p. 532). The result is deteriorating governance and hampered economic development. The confluence of democracy and clientelism directs government activities toward serving the private interests of a corrupt few, turning clientelism and elite entrenchment into self-reinforcing processes. Providing rents through patron-client relationships in exchange for political support is widely regarded as a highly inefficient and growth-retarding form of redistribution (e.g., Robinson and Verdier, 2013). Democracy-first sequences should thus *negatively* influence economic growth according to this argument.

In contrast, when a meritocratic and rule-following bureaucracy is already in place and rule of law is established, the alluring opportunities for clientelism and patronage are shut off for democratic politicians, with benevolent effects on economic outcomes. Countries following such sequences are more likely to follow development paths to "Denmark." In "Denmark," "all three sets of political institutions [are] in perfect balance: a competent state, strong rule of law and democratic accountability" (Fukuyama, 2014a, p. 25). Getting to "Denmark," therefore, requires a favorable historical pathway of institutional development wherein strong state institutions appear before democratization.

Figure 1 outlines the causal chain linking the sequence of institutional adoption to economic growth. The first links are carefully detailed by extant stateness-first arguments cited here; institutional sequencing influences how democracy and state institutions work and thus the wider policymaking environment. Subsequently, the policies selected affect other outcomes – extant contributions such as Fukuyama (2014a) point this out but often without mapping out the final links in detail. Let us therefore detail how the functioning of (democratic and state) institutions may shape the capacity and incentives of politicians to select particular policies, which, in turn, shape the behavior of investors, workers or entrepreneurs. Importantly, all the "immediate" determinants of growth – physical capital, labor hours, human capital, and technology/productivity – are responsive to which economic policies are pursued (e.g., Acemoglu, 2008). Yet, concerning the particular policy features in focus in stateness-first arguments, several studies suggest that they are especially influential for physical capital investments. Let us elaborate.

If democracy-first transitions lead to a policy-environment dominated by instability and short time horizons, as proponents of the stateness-first argument hypothesize, this should mitigate physical capital investments and thus growth (e.g., North, 1990; Olson, 1993; Bizzarro et al., 2018). The profitability of investment projects depend on the wider regulatory framework and investors are often reluctant to invest when they are uncertain about whether relevant policies will change in the future (Rodrik, 1991). Concerning corruption, another supposed ill enhanced by democracy-first transitions, this generates additional costs for investors as well as substantial uncertainty about expected profits. Concerning clientelism, this might incentivize policy makers to expend public funds to provide short-term consumption for particular constituencies, rather than longer-term investments in national infrastructure or other growth-enhancing public goods (e.g., Bueno de Mesquita et al., 2003). Clientelism can also mitigate economic development by reducing productivity growth via inefficient resource allocation (e.g., Robinson and Verdier, 2013). Finally, "democratizing backwards" may impact negatively on broad, national programs that ensure the quality of public services pertaining to education and health care (e.g., D'Arcy and Nistotskaya, 2017), thereby mitigating human capital accumulation.

Before critically addressing different assumptions underlying the stateness-first argument, let us highlight plausible *positive* arguments for why democracy-first transitions could lead to faster, rather than slower, growth, than stateness-first transitions: Albertus and Menaldo (2018) show how high state capacity under autocracy is a prime determinant of what type of democracy is set up, once a transition occurs. Notably, high state capacity reduces chances of transitioning into a "popular democracy," which channels decision-making power to the broader populace and curtails elite power. Instead, high state capacity under autocracy conduces transitions to "gamed democracy." In these formally democratic systems, former autocratic elites *de facto* control power and can – despite extensive suffrage – often veto proposed economic policies and reforms. Economic policies favoring *entrenched* economic elites, in turn, often hamper economic dynamism pertaining to growth of new firms and new sectors and thus productivity growth (e.g., North, 1990; Acemoglu and Robinson, 2012). If building state capacity under autocracy heightens the risk of obtaining an elite-controlled rather than "popular" democracy, this may constitute one channel through which stateness-first transitions mitigate long-term growth.

One notable challenge to the stateness-first argument is raised by Stasavage (2020), who provides a comprehensive account of the rise and fall of pre-modern and modern democracies. Stasavage shows how pre-modern polities with proto-democratic rule was quite common, globally, and that democratic governance structures tended to arise where centralized bureaucracies were absent. In this view, pre-modern democracy and centralized states are sub-stitutes; both can be used – albeit in different ways – by rulers to organize and monitor production, conscript soldiers, and raise taxes. In polities with strong centralized bureaucracies, such as imperial China, rulers did not need the people's consent to govern effectively, while in weaker polities, such as the European city states, leaders required popular participation and legitimacy among key social groups to govern effectively, with positive long-term con-sequences for governance and economic outcomes. Hence, weak states may have been a historical *precondition* for the rise of early democracy in Europe, the first continent on which the "Denmarks" of the world arose.

Another strand of recent work that significantly nuances and casts some doubt on the purported benefits of stateness-first sequences, are several contri-butions by Acemoglu and Robinson (and summarized in their book, Acemoglu and Robinson, 2019). These authors point to multiple historical cases indicat-ing that successful democratization, state building and economic development usually only obtains in a "narrow corridor." In this corridor, the state is always weak enough to be counterbalanced by other forces in civil society (should rul-ing elites attempt to consolidate power in their own hands), but strong enough to prevent the emergence of rule largely by informal local groups, thereby con-straining norms and informal institutions of various kinds (clan governance, mob rule, etc.). If this notion of an intermediately strong state being a precursor of effective democratization and economic development (as well as subsequent, further state building) is correct, then it presents a significant caveat to the stateness-first argument. Embarking on a stateness-first institutional path where state capacity is built very high before attempts at liberalization of the political regime is likely to lead to an aborted sequence of institutional change; democ-racy will never arrive and the country will end up with a consolidated "Despotic Leviathan" generating occasionally high but erratic, rates of economic growth.

3 Taking a Critical Look at the Stateness-First Argument

We propose that the stateness-first argument faces three major hurdles before it can be accepted as firm knowledge. First, the argument is often insufficiently specified. In particular, studies invoking such an argument typically fail to outline the exact counterfactual institutional configurations and development patterns when arguing for the economic (or other) benefits of building state capacity before democratization. What comparisons does the argument rely on? While extant case studies (e.g., Fukuyama, 2014a) and cross-national regressions (e.g., D'Arcy and Nistotskaya, 2017) provide evidence that strong state institutions positively affect development outcomes, they do not really provide evidence for the effect of particular sequences. Second, the stateness-first argument rests on several strong and possibly erroneous assumptions about the relationship between state building and democracy. Third, the stateness-first argument has not been subjected to the same types of stringent and systematic empirical testing as many other propositions on determinants of development. One main reason for this, we believe, has been the lack of extensive time-series data on different, relevant institutional features. This situation has only recently been alleviated, notably with the invention of the V-Dem dataset. Hence, it remains unclear whether the stateness-first argument is valid, even if many scholars and policy makers find it plausible.

3.1 Assumptions and Counterfactuals

We discuss three strong assumptions undergirding the stateness-first argument. They concern the difficulty of building states under democracy, the presumed ease of building states under autocracy, and the likelihood of observing democratic transitions once an autocracy has eventually managed to build a strong state. We are not the first to observe that these are problematic assumptions. Mazzuca and Munck (2014), for example, note that "the argument against 'premature democratization' ... downplays the costs associated with attempts by non-democratic rulers to resolve the question of nation-ness" while it also "exaggerates the negative consequences of democratization by attributing violence to democratization when it is due to the weaknesses of the centre or even to decisions of autocratic rulers" (p. 1232). Let us elaborate on these criticisms in some more detail.

State Building under Democracy: One key assumption of the stateness-first argument is that state building is relatively hard to do in democracies, especially when starting from a low-capacity setting. Yet, Mazzuca and Munck (2014) note that state building and processes of democratization have often coevolved, historically, and that early democratization may even ease nation- and state-building (see also Acemoglu and Robinson, 2019). Democratization presumably provides the state with much-needed legitimacy among contending elites and citizens. Przeworski (1991) points out that democratic institutions may function as a conflict-management device either through allowing for contemporary power sharing or the prospects for regulated alternation of power in the future. This, in turn, mitigates the incentives of contending political elites to pursue armed civil conflict (which has negative consequences for several political and economic development outcomes).

Further, democratically elected leaders face stronger incentives to provide public goods and services (Bueno de Mesquita et al., 2003; Lake and Baum, 2001). Providing public services in an efficient manner may increase reelection chances, thus incentivizing democratic leaders to build a competent bureaucratic apparatus for delivering such services. Public goods and services provision also requires taxation, which, in turn, requires well-functioning bureaucratic support functions. This creates another, albeit indirect, incentive for democratic politicians to build state capacity. Some large-N studies have tested for a relationship between democracy and state capacity, mostly reporting a positive association (Adsera et al., 2003; Carbone and Memoli, 2015; Wang and Xu, 2018). While these findings run counter to a core assumption undergirding the stateness-first argument, some studies have added qualifications, suggesting a J-shaped relationship between democracy and state capacity (Bäck and Hadenius, 2008), that democracy only enhances capacity in rich-country contexts (Charron and Lapuente, 2010), or that competitive elections enhance capacity whereas suffrage has the opposite effect (Andersen and Cornell, 2018).

State Building under Autocracy: A second and related assumption is that autocrats are both able and willing to develop strong and capable state institutions. The empirical findings mentioned in the foregoing paragraph call this notion into question. Notwithstanding the question of whether autocratic regimes have the requisite knowledge and capacity for such institution building, we should ask: how strong are the incentives to invest in state capacity for most autocrats? Indeed, several theoretical contributions imply that autocratic regimes often have strong incentives to *under*-invest in state building, for instance, because this in certain contexts enables leaders to become wealthy or enhance their tenure in power (e.g., Besley and Persson, 2009, 2010; Charron and Lapuente, 2010). To use the terminology of Acemoglu and Robinson, autocrats often have incentives to maintain "Paper Leviathans," as the "lack of state capacity is sometimes a powerful tool in the hands of unscrupulous leaders" (Acemoglu and Robinson, 2019, 345).

Autocrats sometimes even have incentives to "build down" the quality and capacity of state institutions and "informalize" politics, for instance, to enhance personal control over access to public resources (Knutsen, 2013). Studies on political developments in sub-Saharan African countries in the postcolonial period, for instance, have exemplified how some leaders faced these incentives, resulting in a dynamic of autocrats undermining state capacity (e.g., Chabal and Daloz, 1999). While there are situations where autocrats (and democratic leaders) face strong incentives to build state capacity – for instance, presented with an external threat (e.g., Tilly, 1990; Fukuyama, 2014a) – we surmise that most autocratic regimes do not face strong such incentives.

***Democratic Transitions in Consolidated Autocracies*:** A third and often implicit, assumption is that autocratic governments are willing to yield power and oversee transitions to democracy – or, at least, that they are more easily pressured into doing so – after the building of state institutions. This is required for stateness-first regimes to eventually end up like "Denmark." Yet, there is little evidence that autocratic regimes more easily yield power after state building. Instead, autocratic regimes presiding over a state that can effectively extract resources, which may be used (e.g., for co-optation and repression), seem better able to cling to power. Stasavage (2020) presents numerous and detailed historical case studies of autocratic regimes presiding over strong states and that managed to leverage their capable state apparatuses to extract revenue and repress threats. Autocratic regimes in strong states, with different Chinese dynasties being prime examples, managed to rule for extended periods of time, even centuries, without conceding any form of democratization or otherwise breaking down. In fact, Andersen et al. (2014) find that the expansion of fiscal capacity and a firm monopoly on violence significantly prolong autocratic regime durability. Similarly, recent studies find evidence that state capacity moderates the effect of elections on autocratic regime breakdown (Seeberg, 2015; van Ham and Seim, 2017).

Hence, the final step in the stateness-first sequence, democratization, is hard to achieve (and when it eventually comes, the transition may be to an elite-controlled democracy; Albertus and Menaldo, 2018). Countries that build state capacity under autocracy can thus be stuck in a high capacity–autocracy equilibrium – the "Despotic Leviathan" equilibrium, to once again use Acemoglu and Robinson's (2019) terminology – without reaping the anticipated development benefits following a "mature" democratic transition. This means that countries following the prescription of postponing democratization to first build effective state institutions may, in the best-case scenario, end up as Singapore – a high capacity, wealthy nondemocracy – over a prolonged period of time, rather than as "Denmark."

***Specifying the Counterfactual*:** The stateness-first argument is a causal one – building state capacity before democratization causes faster economic development. Like all causal arguments, its validity hinges on assumptions about counterfactuals. What is the relevant comparison to a state that democratized after high-capacity state institutions came in place? (See also Knutsen, 2013.) This question is often neglected or only vaguely addressed in existing contributions, for understandable reasons. Explicitly specifying the appropriate counterfactual in the stateness-first argument is trickier than one might suppose and the counterfactual critically depends on how one interprets the theory.

First, if we interpret the theory to concern the causal effect of democratization D (a binary variable in which $1 = $ democratization), conditional on the preexisting level of state capacity, S ($0 = $ *low*; $1 = $ *high*), on some outcome, Y, the proper comparison is:

$$(Y_{(D=1|S=1)} - Y_{(D=0|S=1)}) - (Y_{(D=1|S=0)} - Y_{(D=0|S=0)}) \qquad (1)$$

This expression compares the effects of democratization in high- vs. in low-capacity states, and the expectation from the stateness-first argument is that it is positive. In this formulation, constructing the counterfactual outcome for a democratizing state under high capacity is non-trivial, since it involves comparing it to three counterfactual scenarios and not simply democratization under low capacity. In Section 6, we approximate such comparisons by using panel regressions (e.g., Figure 14) but also through pre-parametric matching (e.g., Models 1 and 2, Table 2).

Still, some versions of the stateness-first argument focus exclusively on differences within the subset of observations that actually experience democratization. The expectation is that obtaining democracy under high state capacity should lead to stronger future development than democratizing in low-capacity contexts. This is equivalent to stating that

$$Y_{(D=1|S=1)} - (Y_{(D=1|S=0)}) > 0 \qquad (2)$$

While this does not speak to the *causal effect of democratization* – no contrasts are made against counterfactual outcomes associated with remaining autocratic – this descriptive claim certainly exists in various studies promoting stateness-first arguments. We evaluate this claim by only comparing observations that have undergone democratic transitions (e.g., Models 3–5, Table 2).

Yet, if we interpret the stateness-first argument as a theory claiming that the *sequence* of institutional changes matters, the proper comparison is between a country that historically democratized *after* developing a high-capacity state and a country that democratized *before* doing so. Importantly, such comparisons focus on effects of particular *historical sequences* of institutional adoptions and isolates them from the effects of *levels* of state capacity and democracy. The expected pattern should thus presumably be observable also when controlling for the current levels of democracy and state capacity. Yet, as we discuss further for our matching specifications in the following, a country that democratized before building capable state institutions would also, on net, be expected to have high levels of democracy and state capacity at current. Different tests that assess this specification of the theory are presented in Section 6.3.

A final complicating matter for evaluating the stateness-first argument is the complex interrelationship between democracy and state capacity. Several discussions in this and previous sections suggest that state capacity is endogenous to regime type but also that democratization is endogenous to state capacity. These points are appreciated by proponents of the stateness-first argument, although the anticipated signs of the relationships often differ from what our discussions in this section suggest. Nonetheless, if there are links between the two institutional factors, this has implications for counterfactual comparisons and empirical design. If we assume that subsequent regime developments and changes to state capacity are linked to whether or not the first historical transition to democracy took place in a high- or low-capacity context – for instance, because "premature democratization" leads to both political instability and difficulties in state building – we should only compare observations on the basis of their first democratic transition. Further, we should then measure Y with a substantial time lag and *not* control for subsequently realized values on democracy and state capacity, since doing so would induce posttreatment bias (e.g., Model 4, Table 2). In contrast, if we believe further changes to regime type and state capacity (after the first historical transition) are driven mostly by other factors, we should control for these subsequent historical developments and even current realizations of state capacity and democracy (e.g., Model 5, Table 2; Models 3–5, Table 3).

3.2 Extant Evidence

The current evidence-base for the stateness-first argument mostly consists of historical country narratives. Notably, both early (e.g., Huntington, 1968) and recent contributions (e.g., Fukuyama, 2014a) draw on case histories comporting with the prescribed sequence of building state institutions before introducing mass politics, often from Western countries, to support the argument. Yet, Møller (2015) questions the accuracy of the common narrative on sequencing of institutions in Western countries, arguing that

> [t]he notion, so often taken for granted, that it went 'state-first, democracy later,' rests on an oversimplification of European history. What that history shows is that instances of either 'state-first' or 'democracy-first' sequencing were rare. What was much more common was for budding state institutions,

the rule of law and political accountability to grow alongside one another while interacting in messy ways. If there is any sequential pattern, it is for state-building to appear very late in the game. (p. 111)

Responding to this criticism, Fukuyama (2014b) claims that it employs a too-inclusive definition of democracy and that the historical legislative assemblies and rights highlighted by Møller (2015) represent rule-of-law institutions rather than democracy.

This discussion points to a broader problem with the extant case-based evidence for the stateness-first argument: When stringent operationalizations of relevant institutional features are lacking, it is, in practice, difficult to *reliably* describe the actual sequence of institutional development and rigorously compare it to the ideal sequence postulated in the theory. To further illustrate this point, Stasavage (2020) presents detailed historical narratives as well as data on, for instance, tax extraction rates to support the notion that many Western European states (with some exceptions such as Prussia) were actually relatively weak for a long time, especially when compared to China. If true, this further weakens a key premise of the studies claiming empirical evidence for the stateness-first argument from Western European experiences. The lack of stringent operationalizations makes it problematic to assess whether a case narrative – no matter how thorough – actually corroborates the stateness-first argument.

Second, it is hard to systematically control for several factors that contribute to the endogenous evolution of state capacity and democracy in historical narrative designs. We exemplify this point in our case studies of Greece and Denmark in Section 5; there were several features that differentiated these countries other than their differing institutional sequences. Drawing inferences from direct comparisons of such dissimilar cases may therefore easily lead to wrong conclusions.

Third, the previously discussed problem of clearly identifying proper counterfactuals raises issues for the interpretation of case narratives. To evaluate hypotheses on the detrimental consequences of "premature" democratization, the appropriate contrast class for the clientelistic, young democracy with low state capacity and weak rule of law not only includes countries that democratized under strong state capacity and well-functioning rule of law but also the patronage-ridden autocracy with low state capacity and weak rule of law. Such complex comparisons have typically not been made in a systematic manner in the case-based literature.

Finally, when explicit rules for selecting countries are absent, the case-based evidence invites charges of selective choice and interpretation of cases. Despite the numerous case narratives introduced in, for instance, Fukuyama (2014a), an even larger number of relevant cases are lacking. How would, for example, the inclusion of narratives from Botswana or Mauritius – recent development miracles, in countries where democratization occurred under (initially) low levels of state capacity – alter the evaluation of the theory? (For numerous country cases, from different regions, that seem to contrast with the stateness-first argument, see Mazzuca and Munck, 2014.) These issues are compounded by lack of clear criteria for how to select among different time periods, patterns, and events to exemplify a country's development. For example, the relatively authoritarian Prussian regime is (correctly) lauded by several scholars for its ability to modernize the military and state. These experiences have been invoked as evidence for the stateness-first argument (e.g., Fukuyama, 2014a). However, a consideration of more recent German history would highlight how autocratic forces contributed to the country entering into two world wars, with devastating effects on infrastructure, the economy, and human development. This speaks to issues of unclear selection of time period under study: whether or not Prussia/Germany is an unambiguous success story depends on whether we end our investigations in 1885, 1920, 1945, or 1970.

The lack of precision on expected time lags of the proposed effects is thus one reason why it is difficult to assess whether case narratives corroborate the theory. This is relevant for the Greek case. Fukuyama (2014a) writes that "[t]he origins of clientelism in Greece are not hard to find; it is the result of the early arrival of electoral democracy, before a modern state had an opportunity to coalesce" (p. 105). Greece, being a European latecomer in introducing modern state institutions has, however, had opportunities, historically, to build up a strong central administration and mitigate corruption under different spells of autocratic rule. The fact that electoral democracy in Greece has not (yet) solved the issues of clientelistic networks – which Fukuyama also argued were prevalent long before the introduction of democracy – may thus not be considered as unequivocal evidence for the stateness-first argument. Clientelism in current Greece could be understood as the democratic face of a phenomenon that has existed for a long time, irrespective of what regime governed.

Also a few large-N studies speak to stateness-first arguments. Notably, D'Arcy and Nistotskaya (2017) provide a novel justification from rational choice theory for the hypothesis that sequencing state building before democratization enhances governance and public goods provision. They draw on an impressive data collection on state-administered cadasters – "systematically arranged inventories of individual land parcels and land ownership" (p. 2) – for seventy-eight countries back to 1 AD and construct an index of states' monitoring capacity. In several cross-section regressions, they show that countries that scored high at democratization currently outperform countries scoring low at democratization on different outcomes (quality of public services, education expenditures, infant mortality rates). However, D'Arcy and Nistotskaya (2017) do not include countries that remained autocratic in their analysis and consequently do not compare the performance of democratizers versus non-democratizers either in low- or high-capacity contexts. This lack of comparison generates issues for evaluating any causal effect implied by the stateness-first argument. Countries such as Denmark or Sweden, with high capacity at democratization, are associated with better outcomes than countries with low capacity at democratization, such as Benin or Mongolia. But, this finding could stem from other factors, such as state capacity being persistent *and* affecting development (regardless of timing of democratization). Hence, these analyses do not provide direct evidence for the stateness-first argument.

Two studies speak somewhat more directly to the stateness-first argument by investigating whether the effects of democracy are conditional on level of state capacity, with economic growth (Knutsen, 2013) and health care and education (Hanson, 2015) as outcomes. Both studies suggest that democracy actually has a significantly *stronger* positive effect on development outcomes in contexts of low state capacity. These findings contrast with a core assumption undergirding the stateness-first argument, namely that democracy has more benevolent effects in high-capacity contexts. Still, both of these studies rely on fairly limited time series or time-invariant measures of state capacity and they do not explicitly assess historical sequences.

When commenting on the wider literature on the benefits of stateness-first and democratization-first sequences, Mazzuca and Munck (2014) note that "lacking are good tests, using appropriate measures, that empirically adjudicate between these alternative perspectives." We concur and aim to rectify this situation with our analyses in Sections 5 and 6, which employ new, global data with time series comprising most of "modern history." Before we turn to these tests, however, we describe and discuss the data and measures that we use.

4 Measuring Sequences of State Capacity and Democracy

Stateness-first arguments have been difficult to test systematically. This is not only because clearly specified counterfactuals and empirical implications have been lacking, but also due to data limitations. Hypotheses derived from stateness-first arguments pertain to developments over long periods of time and involve different institutions that need to be distinguished. The measures and data required should (a) cover many countries, (b) have long time series, and (c) include detailed and distinct indicators on the relevant institutional features.

Some datasets pertaining to democracy, such as Polity (Marshall and Jaggers, 2007), offer long time series but only include democracy-relevant measures. Measures of state capacity have, until recently, either been cross-sectional (e.g., Evans and Rauch, 1999) or based on short time series covering recent decades (e.g., Kaufmann et al., 2010).

Fortunately, the data situation has improved recently, with several new measures that offer extensive coverage on both democracy and state capacity. A major innovation is the Varieties of Democracy (V-Dem) dataset (see Coppedge et al., 2020a). We primarily rely on data v.10 of V-Dem (Coppedge et al., 2020c), which covers 202 countries and more than 470 indicators. Many of these indicators were recently extended from 1900 and back to the late-eighteenth or early-nineteenth century for up to ninety-one polities – thus covering a key period of democratization and state building in several European, Latin American, and other countries – by Historical V-Dem (Knutsen et al., 2019). This historical data collection also included several new measures of various "Weberian" and other features of state institutions, which have now been extended all the way to the present for most countries.

Some V-Dem indicators – examples being de jure extension of suffrage rights or existence of state institutions such as statistical agencies – are more objective in nature and coded by research assistants. Other measures are more evaluative and require expert judgments. For the latter questions, V-Dem uses numerous expert coders. More than 3,000 country experts have been involved in the data collection, coding surveys on particular subject areas (e.g., elections, parties, state institutions) for countries on which they have in-depth knowledge. V-Dem's norm is to have at least five experts per question for each country for the post-1900 period. For the historical period, where true experts are scarce, fewer expert coders are involved (see Coppedge et al., 2020a; Knutsen et al., 2019).

There are several benefits of using V-Dem's data for measuring the complex concepts of democracy and state capacity. First, V-Dem's country experts can provide case-based knowledge and capture finer details that objective measures may miss. Expert coders can use a range of sources and pieces of evidence when coding and this is appropriate for complex, latent phenomena that are hard to infer from unambiguous observational rules. Second, V-Dem employs item-response theory (IRT) modeling that uses information on, for example, agreement between experts, differences in their coding-thresholds, and self-reported uncertainty to address uncertainty and potential biases. Importantly for our purposes, the consistency of the time series from the historical and post-1900 period is ensured by several operations, which provide information that is fed into the measurement model. These operations include experts coding anchoring vignettes and all (historical and contemporary) coders covering an overlap period of twenty years (typically 1900–20). Third, V-Dem offers unprecedented coverage across countries and time, allowing us to draw on information from back to 1789, before modern democratic and state institutions were developed in most countries.

Nonetheless, one issue with expert-coded measures pertains to the potential for so-called subjectivity biases. For instance, many experts might overestimate countries' performance on both free and fair elections *and* rule-following and impartial administration if they observe very high economic growth. If this particular bias occurs, the panel regressions in Section 6, for example, will over-estimate a positive interaction between democracy and state capacity on growth, thus biasing results *in favor* of the stateness-first argument. While such subjectivity biases are hard to rule out, we find it unlikely that they strongly influence our results. First, the specific nature of the V-Dem questions, formulated to capture more detailed features such as existence of election violence or voter registration records, are presumably less affected by subjectivity bias than broader or vaguer questions. Second, V-Dem uses several country experts and takes methodological safeguards to mitigate coder idiosyncrasies. Nonetheless, to safeguard against our conclusions being affected by subjectivity biases, we also leverage (nonexpert coded) measures on more objective features such as share of population with suffrage rights or state capacity measures that draw on censuses and statistical year-books.

In the following, we discuss how we conceptualize and measure, first, democracy and, second, state capacity. We then employ our main measures to illustrate different historical sequences of institutional adoption in countries across the world.

4.1 Measuring Democracy

We define democracy in a rather narrow and conventional manner, by following Dahl's (1971) electoral concept. Thus, we focus on the institutional conditions that guarantee, first, elite contestation for legislative and executive offices and, second, inclusiveness in determining these contests through broad participation rights. In other words, democracy pertains to the conduct of regular and contested multiparty elections for offices – and minimum prerequisites for making such contests free and fair – as well as extensive political participation rights for the adult population, notably voting rights. Countries become more democratic when contestation *or* participation improves.

This choice of conceptualization is not self-evident; as Coppedge et al. (2011) highlight, the literature contains a plethora of understandings of "democracy." Scholars often add specific dimensions to the core electoral aspects listed here, arguing that a "true democracy" requires more than contested elections and suffrage. Suggested dimensions include guaranteed civil liberties and constraints on the chief executive ("liberal democracy"), direct citizen involvement in civil society and other nonelectoral processes ("participatory democracy"), open and well-functioning deliberation among politicians and citizens ("deliberative democracy") and guarantees of socioeconomic rights and absence of inequalities in economic resources ("egalitarian democracy").

Nonetheless, competitive elections with extensive suffrage remains at the core of modern democracy definitions. Such elections are requisites for "rule by the people" in large, modern states where direct representation and involvement in politics by all adult citizens is infeasible (Dahl, 1998). Moreover, maintaining an electoral definition of democracy carries several benefits for empirical analysis in our particular research context:

First, since we are interested in studying the intricate relationships between democracy, state capacity, and economic development *empirically*, allowing a priori conceptual overlaps would be problematic – this generates correlations by construction. We must therefore shed references to how bureaucracies enforce rules when defining democracy, for example, which a focus on electoral democracy allows us to do. Second, in addition to V-Dem's Polyarchy index introduced below, there are other measures with extensive coverage that rely on an electoral definition of democracy that we can use for robustness tests. Lastly, keeping a narrow focus on the electoral dimension of democracy keeps us in line with the literature that we address and type of argument that we set out to test. The stateness-first arguments that we have reviewed and discussed focus explicitly on the introduction of "mass politics" and on suffrage extensions in particular. More generally, arguments such as those presented by Huntington (1968) and Fukuyama (2014a) highlight the introduction of rather rudimentary expansions of democratic institutions and rights – they do not consider increases in democratic quality from high initial levels of democracy as explanatory variables but rather changes across some (fairly low) electoral democracy threshold.

We use the Polyarchy index from V-Dem (*v2x_polyarchy*) to capture electoral democracy. This index is explicitly modeled on Dahl's conceptualization of democracy, which we here abide by, and the index thus helps us to ensure high concept validity. The indicators included and the aggregation rules used to construct Polyarchy are described in Teorell et al. (2019), but we give a summary here. Polyarchy contains five subcomponents on whether the chief executive and legislature are elected, how free and fair elections are, and the extent of freedom of association, freedom of speech, and universal suffrage. While the latter subcomponent is a single indicator counting the share of the adult population with de jure voting rights, the first four subcomponents are indices. These indices, in turn, consist of several V-Dem indicators, most of which are expert coded. The elected officials index consists of nineteen indicators on whether the chief executive and legislators are elected directly or indirectly or appointed. The free and fair elections index incorporates eight indicators capturing different forms of electoral manipulation and election irregularities. The freedom of association index counts six indicators, for instance, on party bans and civil society repression. Finally, the freedom of expression index aggregates nine indicators. The Polyarchy index is thus a comprehensive measure, capturing various types of institutional guarantees and de facto practices that ensure contested multiparty elections with extensive participation by adult citizens.

While the inclusion of suffrage, elected executives, and free and fair elections are fairly self-evident, the two components capturing civil liberties require some elaboration. Briefly, these civil liberties – in addition to being important features in their own right – are relevant here because they play important "support-functions" for the execution of truly contested elections. More specifically, the inclusion of freedoms of association and speech reflect, respectively, the importance of free formation of opposition parties and open discussion for multiparty elections to be truly competitive (see Dahl, 1971). Without the ability to freely form new parties or the ability to freely criticize government proposals or inform voters about relevant policy alternatives, even elections without open harassment may be less competitive and, in practice, only serve to ensure that incumbent governments are reelected.

The final index is scaled to range, theoretically, from 0 to 1. The empirical minimum and maximum values, for 25,342 country-years, are 0.007 (Guinea-Bissau under Portuguese colonial rule in 1930–32) and 0.924 (Sweden, 2011), respectively. Figure 2 illustrates that most observations cluster on the lower end of the scale, with differences in the middle and higher ends reflecting variation between "minimum electoral democracies" and "high-quality democracies." This skewed distribution also implies that the median value in the sample (0.172; Japan, 1891) is below the mean value (0.263; United Kingdom, 1824) and examples of regimes that fall between the mean and the median value include Germany, 1913, and Iran, 2000. There is substantial over-time variation in Polyarchy scores. For example, the global average increases steadily during Huntington's (1991) "long first wave of democratization" during the nineteenth and early twentieth century, and during the "third wave" starting in the mid-1970s. Despite several periods of stagnation and "reverse democratization

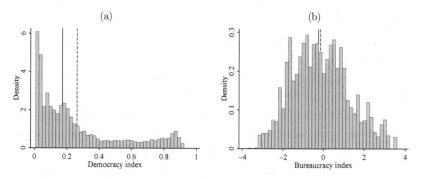

Figure 2 Distributions of scores for Polyarchy (a) and impartial and rule-following administration (b, *v2clrspct*), 1789–2019. Dotted/solid line represents mean/median.

waves," notably in the 1930s and early 1940s, the mean score by the end of the time series (0.52 in 2019) was far higher than in 1789 (0.06).

Democracy scholars continue to disagree over where to (most appropriately) draw the line between democracies and nondemocracies (Bogaards, 2012). Where possible, we rely on the continuous version of Polyarchy and thereby avoid using inevitably arbitrary thresholds. Still, several analyses require dichotomous measures. The categorical "Regimes of the World" measure contained in V-Dem, somewhat simplified, uses a 0.5 cut-off on Polyarchy to distinguish democracies from nondemocracies (for details, see Lührmann et al., 2018). This 0.5 cut-off is mainly devised to distinguish contemporary electoral democracies from electoral authoritarian regimes. For our purposes, the 0.5 threshold is not viable for comparing countries historically. According to this threshold, no country was democratic before 1849 (Switzerland, 0.55) and several crucial cases that Fukuyama and Huntington count as democracies and use to support their arguments count as autocracies. Polyarchy's average global mean was consistently below 0.25 before 1900 and only reached 0.5 in 2001.

Stateness-first arguments have, as noted, focused on the introduction of core, minimum-level democratic institutions and rights. We therefore use relatively low cut-off values to dichotomize Polyarchy. As a benchmark, we divide Polyarchy by its median value (0.172 in the full sample), which produces evenly split subsamples and thus ensures higher-powered tests. In robustness tests, we dichotomize Polyarchy by the sample mean (0.263). We also try out different cut-offs, including the 0.5 threshold. Further, we test the binary electoral democracy measure from Boix et al. (2012, BMR), which registers the presence of free and fair elections and requires that 50 percent of adult men are enfranchised. Appendix Figure A.2 shows the number of democracies according to the different measures and operational rules mentioned here, and Appendix Figure A.1 show the Polyarchy value for all countries in our sample. Given the emphasis put on suffrage in stateness-first arguments, we also run tests with V-Dem's *v2x_suffr* indicator instead of a composite democracy measure.

4.2 Measuring State Capacity

We conceptualize "state capacity" as the ability of state institutions to implement (various) policies, as envisioned by those who drafted these policies and across the state's territory, even when social actors oppose the implementation of these policies. Several authors consider state capacity to be a multidimensional concept (e.g., Fukuyama, 2004), as capacity may vary across policy areas and be specific to different substantive tasks such as employing violence, gathering information, or taxing citizens. Yet, at the abstract level, the concept has a common core – the notion that states can effectively implement whatever policies policymakers decide on – regardless of whether we consider the capacity to collect taxes or implement other policies. Along these lines, Lindvall and Teorell propose that state capacity, generally, "can be defined as the strength of the causal relationship between the policies that governments adopt and the outcomes that they intend to achieve" (Lindvall and Teorell, 2016, 1). Some of the alternative measures used in Sections 5 and 6 are, indeed, of the more specific kind, including a measure on states' capacity to collect information (Brambor et al., 2019). Yet, given the nature of the stateness-first argument – with a proposed relevance of capable and effective state institutions, more generally, being built before democratization – we mainly use measures that do not differentiate across policy areas or different state tasks.

Instead, we largely rely on measures that capture a key requisite for states being effective in implementing (various kinds of) policies, namely the makeup of the state bureaucracy. Bureaucracies are the machineries that states use to implement tax reforms, collect information, and ensure citizen compliance with different laws across the land. We thus follow the widely held assumption that there are strong correlations between several, particular bureaucratic features and state capacity. This assumption is crucial, insofar as state capacity conceptualized as the power to implement policies and achieve intended outcomes is inherently unobservable.

More specifically, the bureaucratic features that we conceive as vital for achieving high state capacity, and which we measure empirically, relate to Max Weber's ideal notion of a bureaucracy (Weber, 1968). In brief, Weber's ideal bureaucracy is a hierarchical organization where lines of authority and areas of responsibility are clearly delineated. Further, decisions are arrived at via applying clearly codified rules, rather than officials using personal discretion, and decision-making is conducted in an impartial manner. Moreover, bureaucrats should have decent salaries, which presumably makes them less dependent on political patrons and less likely to engage in corruption. Finally, the officials staffing the bureaucracy should be recruited and promoted according to merit, rather than other criteria such as personal connections or status. When these criteria are met, we assume that the bureaucracy's ability to effectively implement and enforce various laws and other tasks is comparatively high.

Our main measure for capturing state capacity is selected because of this link between Weberian bureaucratic features and state capacity. Other measures proposed in the literature have relied on different "outcomes," for example, taking taxes as share of GDP or the share of tax revenue coming from nontrade taxes as indicators of state capacity. Various such measures of state capacity are strongly interrelated (Fortin-Rittenberger, 2014), and Hanson and Sigman (2019) therefore use Bayesian methods on multiple measures to derive latent estimates of state capacity back to 1960. We use these latent estimates for robustness tests. Yet, to properly test the stateness-first argument, we require measures with longer time series. Fortunately, recent versions of V-Dem provide several relevant measures of state bureaucracies. V-Dem's reliance on country experts is particularly helpful for constructing valid measures on this concept. Expert coders can use a range of sources and different pieces of evidence to score latent phenomena, such as state capacity, that are hard to capture by a handful of unambiguous observational rules.

Since different aspects of Weberian bureaucracy are relevant for influencing state capacity, we opt for a measure with extensive coverage and that captures core elements of the Weberian ideal. Hence, our main measure is *v2clrspct*, which scores the extent to which public officials are impartial and rule-following in carrying out their duties. We henceforth refer to this indicator as "impartial and rule-following administration." It draws on the responses of country experts to the following question "Are public officials rigorous and impartial in the performance of their duties?" (Coppedge et al., 2020c, 164) and the accompanying clarification highlights that experts should consider "the extent to which public officials generally abide by the law and treat like cases alike or conversely, the extent to which public administration is characterized by arbitrariness and biases (i.e., nepotism, cronyism or discrimination)." As such, this indicator taps into two core characteristics of Weber's ideal bureaucracy, namely that administrative decisions follow clearly specified rules *and* that decisions are implemented in an impersonal manner.

Country experts originally score this item on a five-point ordinal scale, ranging from "[T]he law is not respected by public officials. Arbitrary or biased administration of the law is rampant" to "[T]he law is generally fully respected by the public officials. Arbitrary or biased administration of the law is very limited." These scores are subsequently transformed to a continuous scale by the V-Dem measurement model and aggregated across experts for a given country-year. The final measure covers 26,416 country-year observations for 1789–2019. The measurement model–corrected continuous scale ranges from −3.73 (Afghanistan, 1993) to 3.61 (Denmark, 2010) and it is close to normally distributed with a median of −0.24 (Malaysia, 2013) and mean of 0.14 (Bahrain, 1950). The average global score has varied over time and generally displays a gradual, positive trend – the mean value was −0.58 in 1789 (60 countries) and 0.28 in 2019 (179 countries). The right panel of Figure 2 shows the distribution of the full sample.

We use alternative measures for robustness tests, including country-expert coded measures from V-Dem on bureaucratic recruitment and promotion criteria (*v2stcritrecadm*) and remuneration of bureaucrats (*v2strenadm*). The former indicator on recruitment and promotion criteria is particularly useful, as it presumably taps into the competencies and skills of everyday bureaucrats implementing, monitoring, and enforcing laws and decisions. The question posed to V-Dem country experts reads "[T]o what extent are appointment decisions in the state administration based on personal and political connections, as opposed to skills and merit?" (Coppedge et al., 2020b, 178). Once again, experts score countries on a five-point ordinal scale and are asked explicitly to consider the actual practices in the bureaucracy. Further, experts are asked to take a comprehensive view by noting that "[I]f there are large differences between different branches of the state administration or between top and lower level state administrators please try to consider the average when answering the question" (p. 178). Hence, also the meritocratic recruitment indicator is well-suited for a general measure that reflects state capacity in different policy areas and across different tasks that state institutions perform.

We also run tests where we zoom in on states' capacities in particular areas. We use, for instance, V-Dem's expert-coded measure of fiscal capacity (*v2stfisccap*), which may be particularly relevant when economic growth is the dependent variable. This indicator asks experts to consider the sources of revenue that states may draw on, arranged on an ordinal scale according to which revenue sources require relatively more capacity to extract (with, e.g., loans and foreign aid requiring less capacity and income- and sales taxes requiring more). We also test a measure of information capacity (Brambor et al., 2019), which is constructed as a latent estimate from an IRT model drawing on data from more objective indicators coded by research assistants. The particular institutions and tasks scored by the different indicators include the presence/absence of censuses, statistical agencies, and statistical yearbooks.

4.3 Conceptualizing and Measuring Sequences

When measuring historical sequences of institutional adoption in Section 6.3, we use information about the placement of observations relative to the sample medians for both democracy and state capacity, referring to above-median values as "high" and below-median values as "low." Doing so allows us to visualize and compare (albeit crude) patterns of historical-institutional development in a simplified manner. Figure 3 illustrates the transition probabilities, from year $t - 1$ to year t, between each state (i.e., combination of low/high institutional values). The number in each box indicates the proportion of observations in a given state at time $t - 1$ that remained in that state in the following year, and the number to the right of each arrow denotes the proportion that moved to another state. These frequencies show that countries starting out with below-median values on both state capacity and democracy (a "low capacity–low democracy" state) were more likely to develop above-median levels of democracy before capacity than developing high state capacity before high democracy. Nearly 3 percent of low capacity–low democracy observations switched to low capacity–high democracy in the next year, but less than 1 percent switched to high capacity–low democracy. This observation supports our criticism of the stateness-first assumption on state building in autocracies; empirically, few autocracies experience improvements in state capacity that take them beyond the median-threshold on the impartial and rule-following administration measure. We find similar patterns when applying our alternative measures of state capacity.

Still, low capacity–high democracy observations were about four times more likely to revert back to being low on both than high capacity–low democracy observations. This observation is more in line with the stateness-first argument – weak-capacity democracies fairly often "de-democratize." However, this pattern is also consistent with various other theories of political development, including those proposing that low income (which correlates with low state capacity) destabilizes democracies (e.g., Inglehart and Welzel, 2005; Przeworski and Limongi, 1997). Further, the likelihood of transitioning to the "high–high" state is about similar (around 3 percent in $t + 1$) for high capacity–low democracy countries *and* low capacity–high democracy ones; empirically, experiences of state building under democracy is not as infrequent as the stateness-first argument suggests. Finally, the high capacity–high

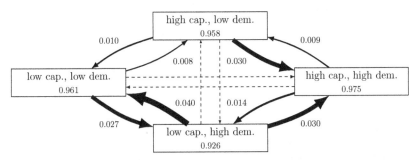

Figure 3 Relative transition probabilities from each state. The four boxes represent the four different combinations of low vs. high scores on both state capacity and democracy. The number in each box shows the proportion of observations in a given state at time $t - 1$ that remained in that state in the following year. The black arrows and corresponding number denotes the proportion that moved to another state. Proportions, which are very low, are not shown for the dotted lines.

democracy state is the most stable one, with almost 98 percent of observations retaining this state in $t + 1$. Once countries get to "Denmark" they tend to stay there. Further, most countries get to "Denmark" via one of two paths. That is, they achieve relatively high levels of both democracy and state capacity by following either a stateness-first *or* a democracy-first trajectory – less than 0.5 percent of observations transitioned directly from low–low to high–high. In Section 6.3, we consider whether following a particular such path matters for subsequent economic development.

To be as inclusive as possible, our initial criteria for classifying countries do not require that transitions between the different institutional states are consecutive but merely that a high capacity–low democracy state [low capacity–high democracy] was observable *before* high capacity–high democracy status occurred to be coded as a stateness-first [democracy-first] sequence. When using these criteria, we count eighty-three "stateness-first" countries (see Appendix Figure A.3). They include countries with high-growth track records, such as Denmark, Japan, and Norway, but also countries with more mixed development records, such as Afghanistan and Egypt. There are fifty-seven "democracy-first" countries; Greece, Morocco, and Argentina are examples.

Figure A.4 in the Appendix shows the institutional trajectories associated with countries that did not go through either a stateness-first or democracy-first pattern of institutional development. There are thirty-one "right-censored" countries that never attained above-median levels of both democracy and state capacity, including the Democratic Republic of Congo, El Salvador, Kazakhstan, and Laos. There are also twenty-eight "left-censored" countries that

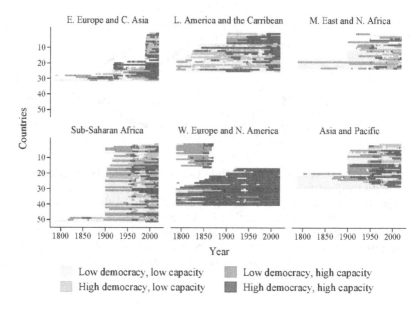

Figure 4 Institutional sequences by region.

entered the sample with high levels of both democracy and capacity or, alternatively, that transitioned to this (high–high) state directly from low levels of both democracy and state capacity. For many countries, especially in Europe and Latin America, the starting year is 1789 or early in the nineteenth century, but for many African and Asian colonies it is 1900. Figure 4 elaborates on differences in institutional sequences in our global sample by plotting the institutional sequence histories of countries by region.[3]

Evaluating patterns by region reveals several notable trends. For one, the vast majority (21/28) of left-censored cases – those that entered the sample with above-median values of both democracy and state capacity – belong to Western Europe and North America. Still, among countries in Western Europe and North America, the most common pattern of development involved stateness-first development (16/40). In contrast, democracy-first development was the most common pattern in Eastern Europe (including the post-Soviet space) (13/31). Many, but not all, of these cases emerged with the fall of the Soviet Union in 1991. Further, stateness-first development has been equally likely as democracy-first development in Latin America; eleven countries are represented in each category. Elsewhere in the so-called "developing world" the

---

[3] See also Table A.1 in the Appendix.

most common pathway was actually stateness-first development. This institutional sequence history characterizes 25/51 countries in sub-Saharan Africa and 15/29 in Asia and the Pacific. In contrast, seventeen sub-Saharan African countries and eight Asian-Pacific countries experienced democracy-first sequences. In the Middle East and North Africa, 85 percent of non-censored cases – eleven versus two – belonged to the stateness-first group; nine countries in this still relatively autocratic region have never attained above-median values on democracy.

5 Case Studies: Greece and Denmark

The histories of Greece and Denmark serve to illustrate two different institutional sequences – democracy-first and stateness-first, respectively – and development patterns. Denmark established a highly professional bureaucracy during its absolutist monarchy in the eighteenth and nineteenth centuries, before embarking on democratization, with the 1848 revolution as a first, key step and then subsequent democratization in the early twentieth century. Today, Denmark is one of the richest, most egalitarian and happiest (according to surveys) countries in the world. Greece, on the other hand, won independence, introduced representative government and started building a bureaucracy around the same time in the nineteenth century. It is presently relatively poor compared to other EU members, and the country has, even recently, experienced widespread corruption, budgetary malpractices, high public debt, and general economic distress.

As Fukuyama (2014a) alludes to, the contrast between these two countries could be used to illustrate the superiority of a stateness-first development path, where the bureaucracy – as in Denmark – is first professionalized under autocratic rule before democracy is introduced. However, we demonstrate how this approach to drawing inferences about the effects of stateness-first sequences is highly problematic. Differences in Greek and Danish history are plentiful, far beyond their different institutional sequences. Hence, the two countries are not well-suited for a structured comparison. To gain more leverage on whether institutional sequencing is *the* important feature that explains differences in economic development, one should, instead, more systematically draw on information from several countries to account for alternative explanations for differences in development.

5.1 Greece

The modern political history of Greece represents a case where core democratic institutions were adopted before an impersonal bureaucracy with merit-based recruitment being established. Greece was among the first countries outside Western Europe that won independence and soon after imported Western institutions. Indeed, Greece adopted institutions such as universal male suffrage long before they were common in Western Europe. Simultaneously, the country's modern history is often presented as a story of failure, beleaguered by misfit institutions imposed by the Ottoman Empire and then dominated by other foreign powers, producing a state bureaucracy that lacked legitimacy in its own population (Fukuyama, 2014a, pp. 94–107, 198–213). However, we immediately note that Greece's modern history could also be presented as a success story, if we adopt a different set of contrasts than Western European countries. The country is today among the most prosperous in its neighborhood. It also displays a decently functioning rule of law when compared to other countries in the region, a fairly modern infrastructure and a population that enjoys a quality of life exceeding most countries in world (Kalyvas, 2015, p. 1).

In line with the theoretical focus on initial democratization experiences, we take the nineteenth century as the defining era of Greek democratization (and state building). Hence, our narrative account extends from Greece's War of Independence with the Ottoman Empire in 1821 until the coup of 1909.

The Greek economy was in a dismal state when the War of Independence broke out. Agricultural productivity had declined during the eighteenth century, at least partly caused by the failing central administration in the Ottoman Empire. When the War of Independence erupted in 1821, it caused further widespread destruction and the Greek population declined by 20 percent during the war. When peace was reached and a constitution adopted in 1832, Greece was in an even more dismal state. It had a huge foreign debt and a population largely consisting of (mostly illiterate) subsistence farmers (Kalyvas, 2015, pp. 18, 37, 58–59). Data from the updated version of the Maddison project (see Bolt and van Zanden, 2013) estimates Greek real GDP per capita in 1833 to 1323 USD (measured in 2011 prices), less than half of the United States' level and substantially lower than the level of Denmark (1790 USD).

Greek efforts in the War of Independence were helped by foreign intervention by the British, French, and Russians. The Greek state was officially formed with the Treaty of Constantinople of 1832 and its political system was structured as an absolute monarchy. The crown was offered to a seventeen-year-old Bavarian prince, Otto I of Greece. To aid the young king in ruling, power was also entrusted to a "troika" of Bavarian regents who would create or reorganize the state administration, nature of taxation, status of religion and the church, and systems of education, justice and city planning. Some changes came quickly; in 1834, Greece became one of the first states to introduce compulsory primary education. Although only about 20 percent would be enrolled in primary education by 1870 (Benavot and Riddle, 1988, p. 205), American records show that three quarters of the Greeks who migrated to the United States between 1900 and 1914 were literate (Kalyvas, 2015, p. 41). The Orthodox Church was changed to a national Church and no longer subordinate to the Patriarchate of Constantinople. The church played a central part in administration and in establishing a national identity. The new legal system completely removed Ottoman law and traditional practices, and the opening of the first Greek university ensured an abundant supply of law school graduates, which helped enable a "legalization" of the administration. By 1907, the number of civil servants per capita was roughly seven times higher than in Britain (Kalyvas, 2015, p. 60).

Despite these reforms toward a modern state administration and political system, the post-independence period is seen by many contemporary Greeks as "colonialism in disguise" (Kalyvas, 2015, p. 39). Indeed, there were several rebellions in the country throughout the 1830s and 40s, and severe tensions developed between local Greeks native to the liberated provinces and foreign-educated, intellectual Greeks. With the expanding state bureaucracy, government jobs became part of a spoils system that spurred intense competition between such factions and hindered the development of an impersonal and impartial public administration (Kalyvas, 2015, p. 38). For example, mass conscription was introduced in 1837, but became ridden with corrupt draft evasion. This type of clientelism is often mentioned explicitly by proponents of the stateness-first thesis (e.g., Fukuyama, 2014a) as a danger of "premature democratization"; in this regard, Greece fits the overall narrative. Yet, we highlight that such clientelist practices existed in Greece long before democratization occurred, although we cannot know whether extended suffrage entrenched the practice or not. (To conclude with certainty, we would need reliable information on how Greek bureaucracy would have developed in the counterfactual situation where suffrage was not extended).

The tensions between different factions in the young Greek state climaxed in 1843 when King Otto tried to cut military spending and was met by a military coup. This event did not end King Otto's rule but spurred the introduction of a French-style constitution. Subsequently, in 1847, near-universal male suffrage was introduced. Thus, barely ten years after independence, Greece became a democratic constitutional monarchy and among the most progressive political regimes in Europe. This is also when Greece first passes our median-Polyarchy threshold, which we use in subsequent analyses to dichotomize relatively autocratic from relatively democratic regimes. However, elections were ridden with fraud and violence, and the Monarch retained extensive executive and legislative power. Ultimately, King Otto was overthrown in another coup in 1862 and the new provisional government invited the Danish prince George to become

Head of State. Many sources therefore treat the constitution of 1864 as the beginning of the Greek democracy (Boix et al., 2012; Kammas and Sarantides, 2020).

The constitution of 1844 did not lead to a full-blown parliamentarian system right away. Like in many other nineteenth-century European countries, the power balance between parliament and crown remained contentious and unresolved. Both King Otto and the subsequent King George would invite loyal minority governments to rule, undermining the parliamentary principle. Only in 1875, did parliament win the power-struggle with the crown, thereby further enhancing the democratic nature of the political system.

Suffrage extension led to a complete transformation of the Greek tax system, shifting government revenue from direct, agricultural taxes toward indirect, urban and market-based taxes. In 1833–44, 66 percent of tax revenue came from agricultural taxes. By 1880–1915, this share was down to 17 percent and taxes were by then primarily extracted from customs (39 percent) and market products (38 percent) (Kammas and Sarantides, 2020). Furthermore, the change to parliamentarism seemingly had fairly quick and positive implications for the country's economy. From 1880 to 1895, there were massive investments in infrastructure, associated first and foremost with Prime Minister Harilaos Trikoupis, who led several governments from 1875 to 1895. From 1882 to 1890, the road network expanded from 1,359 to 5,221 km and the railroad network from 19 to 1,300 km. In 1889, estimated real GDP per capita of Greece was 2,058 USD (2011 prices), up from 1,661 in 1875. However, the massive new investments, together with political and economic reforms, multiplied the country's public expenditures, which, in turn, increased Greece's debt from 331 million drachma in 1882, to 823 million in 1893. In 1893, the government defaulted for the fourth time (1826, 1843, 1860) (Kalyvas, 2015, pp. 63–65), and by the turn of century, Greek GDP per capita was almost back to its 1875 level. Nonetheless, while the economy and state finances were in deep trouble, it is worth remembering that the country had won independence, massively expanded suffrage, established parliamentarism, built the foundations of a bureaucracy, and created the infrastructure for a modern economy in less than eighty years.

A central goal of independent Greece was territorial expansion, known to history as "The Great Idea." Similar to nationalists elsewhere in Europe, Greek leaders considered their nation as much larger than its territories. The desire for territorial expansion channeled money away from domestic projects and toward military expenditures, which typically accounted for 30–40 percent of the Greek state budget. These massive expenditures and emphasis on the armed forces also increased the importance of the military in Greek politics. Regarding fighting capacity, however, the Greek military remained relatively weak.

When Greece annexed the Ionian Islands in 1864 and Thessaly in 1881, it was thanks to clever diplomacy. Yet, the military remained an important domestic political actor. In 1909, a new military coup led to several liberal revisions of the constitution. While Greek history continued to be tumultuous and filled with regime changes – notably with a successful coup in 1967 and subsequent military junta rule until 1974 – we end our story here. The structure of the Greek (modern) democracy had by then been established.

In the relatively short time period under study, Greece underwent an economic and political transformation. How successful these developments were – and the overall interpretation of Greece as a "failure" – hinges on the benchmarks we set for success, what the relevant contrast cases are, and exactly when we measure the parameters of success. Further, the extent to which we can attribute the failures (and successes) of Greece to its particular *sequence* of democratization and state building remains highly unclear, as several other aspects of the Greek context seem about equally likely to constitute key, underlying determinants of the country's development trajectory (e.g., the relationship with the Ottomans and destructive War of Independence, the short time span of institution building, the stark social cleavages, and the ever-present role of the military and foreign governments).

Figure 5 shows four relevant V-Dem measures across 1822–1939 in Greece: Polyarchy capturing overall electoral democracy, suffrage, impartial and rule-following administration, and meritocratic recruitment and promotion to the public administration. The pre-1822 scores capture the situation in Greece under Ottoman rule, illustrating the absence of suffrage and democracy and lack of meritocratic recruitment and promotion practices in the bureaucracy. The public administration was, according to V-Dem expert coders, faring somewhat better on impartiality and ability or willingness to follow clearly codified rules but was still far from exemplary (around median value in the global sample).

With independence comes a modest, but still marked, improvement both in democracy level and meritocratic recruitment, albeit impartial and public administration did not improve. After independence, the three important governmental reforms described in our case study – the introduction of constitutional monarchy, male universal suffrage, and then the introduction of parliamentarism – are associated with notable increases in Greece's Polyarchy-value. As noted, there is initially no development in the measure on rule-following and impartial public administration, however, and the score even drops somewhat as Greece secedes from the Ottoman Empire. The level of meritocratic recruitment, in contrast, improves substantially after Ottoman rule, but thereafter remains stable at the postindependence level, indicating the lack of further progress on a key indicator of state capacity.

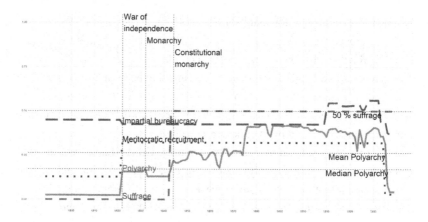

Figure 5 History of Greek institutions. The values prior to 1822 are from the Ottoman Empire.

Regarding the categorization of institutional states and sequences outlined in Section 4, Panel A of Appendix Figure B.1 shows that Greece comports with a democracy-first sequence. The expansion of suffrage in 1847, and the corresponding increase in Polyarchy, results in Greece being coded as having achieved above-median levels of democracy at relatively low levels of state capacity. The increase in the measure of impartial bureaucracy that occurred much later, in 1910, represents its transition to a "high–democracy, high–capacity" state. Hence, when using the categorization scheme outlined in Section 4, Greece is a democracy-first case. In the ensuing century, Greece vacillated between different institutional states, for instance reverting to a low–low state with the restoration of monarchy in 1935 and during the military junta rule in the late 1960s and 1970s. The country has, over the last few decades, once again been in a high-high state. In Appendix Figure B.3, we illustrate how (dis)similar the sequencing history of Greece and Denmark are to all countries in our sample.

5.1.1 Synthetic Control

It is extremely difficult to make informed guesses about what would have happened with Greek political and economic development trajectories if Greece were to have postponed democratization a few decades, after having built a strong state. Nonetheless, researchers sometimes rely on case studies, such as the short one of Greece in Section 5.1, to draw inferences about the effects of particular historical-institutional sequences. In the next section, we present a similar brief case study of Denmark, which established an impartial bureaucracy with merit-based recruitment before introducing democracy.

By directly comparing Denmark and Greece, one might get the impression that the Danish stateness-first sequence is superior to the Greek sequence in producing economic development, since present-day Denmark is far wealthier than current Greece.

We strongly advise against drawing such inferences from these comparisons. The differences between Denmark and Greece are manifold, and it is heroic to identify the sequencing of institutions as *the* most important causally operative difference when explaining the countries' divergent economic development trajectories. For example, Denmark started with the economic structure of a relatively successful empire and several well-established institutions, including a national church, to help build its bureaucracy. Denmark admittedly lost areas of its Empire to other countries but always maintained control over its core and most productive provinces. Greece, on the other hand, started out with an underdeveloped area with only subsistence productivity and a large foreign debt, and built a state from these resources while simultaneously doubling its geographical size. So while one could highlight differences in development between Denmark and Greece today and attribute those to different historical institutional sequences, we could just as well highlight how *similar* the countries are today given how different they were when they embarked upon their processes of state building and democratization.

When facing the dilemma of limited observations and several plausible explanations, one response is to expand the number of data points. In our situation, that would imply adding more case studies that resemble and differ from Greece and Denmark in various, relevant regards. But as the number of plausible alternative explanations increases, it becomes increasingly difficult to keep track of all the details and clearly isolate the signal from the noise. When the number of relevant explanations *and* observations increase, statistics becomes a helpful tool for identifying patterns and drawing valid and reliable inferences. Here, we use the synthetic control method (Abadie et al., 2015) to help us evaluate the effect of Greece's "democracy-first" institutional sequencing history on economic development.

We draw on the estimates of real GDP per capita (p.c.) from the extensive dataset constructed by Fariss et al. (2017) and economic growth, our dependent variable, is measured on an annual basis as the percentage share increase in real GDP p.c. from one year to the next. The synthetic control method works by creating a hypothetical country, "Greece," which we subsequently use as a counterfactual comparison to real Greece. "Greece" and Greece are quite similar in different regards that are relevant for economic development. But, in contrast to Greece, "Greece" does not experience democratization. The method works by using information from all other countries, globally, to find a mix of observations that can reliably predict the GDP p.c. of Greece, prede-mocratization. After democratization, the observed trajectory in GDP p.c. of Greece is then compared to the predicted trajectory in GDP p.c. of "Greece." "Greece" is therefore a *synthetic* alternative to the history for Greece – a simu-lation of a counterfactual scenario based on information from a mix of relevant comparison-countries.

Following our rule on dichotomization of regimes, using the median sample-value on Polyarchy as threshold, we identify 1844 as the year of democratiza-tion for Greece. To construct "Greece," we rely on four variables, namely initial ln GDP p.c. (from Fariss et al. 2017), impartial and rule-following bureaucracy (from V-Dem), ethnic heterogeneity (from Alesina et al. 2003), and geograph-ical region (from V-Dem). In this first analysis, we restrict comparisons (i.e., the countries that we use to construct "Greece") to only include information from the exact same time period as when Greece democratized, namely 1844. We relax this restrictive assumption later on and thus compare Greece to a synthetic control made up of similar countries from different time periods. Yet, in the first analysis when we only draw information from nondemocra-tizers in 1844, "Greece" is predicted based on three other countries: Poland, Egypt, and Nejd/Saudi Arabia.[4] Egypt and Saudi Arabia each contribute 49 percent to "Greece," and Poland only 1 percent. To corroborate the stateness-first hypothesis, the results from the synthetic control analysis would need to show that, after Greece democratizes, it's economic growth is slower than that of "Greece."

Results are illustrated in Figure 6, with the *x*-axis indicating year and the *y*-axis capturing the difference in ln GDP p.c. between Greece and "Greece." When the solid black line is above (below) the dashed horizontal line, located at 0, Greece has a higher (lower) GDP p.c. than "Greece." One important first consideration is whether the pre-1844 trajectories of economic development for Greece and "Greece" are similar. That is, the solid line should be as close as possible to 0 in the ten-year time period before democratization. A large pre-democratization discrepancy would indicate that the constructed "Greece" is not a very good counterfactual for Greece. However, the solid line is close to 0 before 1844, suggesting that "Greece" is, indeed, a good counterfactual.

Greece does experience a dip in GDP per capita right after the change in constitution in 1844, when the country for the first time is scored with an

---

[4] During the nineteenth century, different polities and groups dominated different parts of the area today known as Saudi Arabia. To be precise, the particular historical polity that Historical V-Dem experts code during this time period and which Greece therefore is compared to in our analysis, is the Emirate of Nejd (for a brief introduction, see, e.g., Acemoglu and Robinson, 2019, chapter 12).

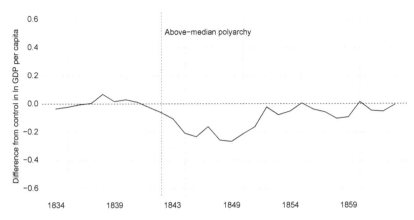

Figure 6 The difference in ln GDP p.c. between Greece and "Greece" from 10 years before to 20 years after democratization.

above-median Polyarchy value. This short-term dip is consistent with the finding from existing regression-based studies (e.g., Papaioannou and Siourounis, 2008) that democratization episodes lead to slower growth in the very short term (but not after a few years have passed). Figure 6 shows that around ten years after democratization, Greece is back on the same trajectory as "Greece" but it remains just below the 0 mark. In other words, our data show a stagnant post-1844 economy in Greece, but does not give any clear evidence of a long-term negative effect of democratization.

With its royal ties, Greece was arguably more interwoven in European politics – the area of the world with the fastest economic development and state building during this time period – than both Egypt and Nejd/Saudi Arabia. Furthermore, Egypt's population was much larger than that of Greece and Egypt also had far more meritocratic recruitment criteria in 1844. Granted, both Nejd and Egypt, like Greece, neighbored the Ottoman Empire and struggled to stay autonomous, although Egypt in reality enjoyed large autonomy. Yet, these countries may not look like the most relevant matches. One problem with the strategy for constructing this synthetic control is that there are few alternative countries that are good candidate matches in the exact same period. Similar late-modernizing countries in Europe were not yet independent *or* they experienced democratization in the same period and can therefore not be used in the synthetic control.

We therefore repeated the synthetic control estimation but removed the restriction that countries contributing to "Greece" must be from the same time period (1834–63). Thus, we trade off similarity in one respect (time period) to achieve more substantive similarity on other relevant variables (income, initial state capacity, ethnic heterogeneity, and geographical region). With this more

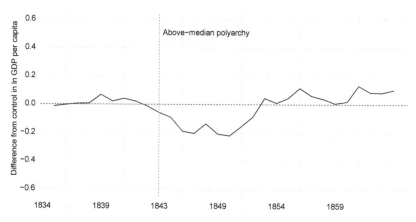

Figure 7 The difference in ln GDP p.c. between Greece and "Greece" from 10 years before to 20 years after democratization, allowing the countries in the synthetic control to be from other 30-year periods than 1834–63.

flexible specification, the synthetic control method composes "Greece" to be a combination of Portugal 1826–55 (70 percent), Spain 1791–1820 (24 percent), Australia 1794–1823 (2 percent), UAE 1971–2000 (2 percent), and Qatar 1950–79 (1 percent). Results from this analysis are presented in Figure 7, and turn out to be very similar to the first analysis. The figure, naturally, shows the same postdemocratization recession in Greece but Greece is now expected to have somewhat *higher* ln GPD p.c. after the first decade than "Greece."

Still, one may reasonably interject that the political regime in Greece after 1844 was not very democratic, indicating that our choice of median score on Polyarchy might be a too liberal operationalization of what constitutes a democracy. We therefore repeated the synthetic control analysis, but this time assume that the true moment of democratization in Greece first came with the introduction of parliamentarism, setting the threshold level for democracy to Greece's 1875 score. Details from this analysis are placed in the Appendix Section B, but results are similar to those here.

To sum up, there is no evidence of any long-term negative effect of democratization in our democracy-first case of Greece across different synthetic control specifications. Hence, we find little systematic evidence in support of a main implication of the stateness-first argument. Yet, the question remains whether the stateness-first argument is right in predicting that democratization enhances growth when happening in a "mature" state with high capacity.

5.2 Denmark

Denmark established a fairly competent, impartial bureaucracy before adopting democratic institutions. The relevant time period of Danish history starts with the absolutist monarchy in 1660, as major developments toward the modern state of Denmark are often attributed to reforms occurring under absolutism. In 1848, absolutism was replaced by a constitutional monarchy, with several key developments affecting the democratic nature of the regime. The post-1848 period was characterized by a constitutional tension over the king's power to appoint the government – the parliamentary principle – which ended in a victory for the parliament in 1901. Modern Danish democracy is often considered to be introduced with the events in 1901. However, 1901 is not characterized by a major suffrage expansion. Rather, 1901 marks the establishment of (negative) parliamentarism and Denmark adopted full universal suffrage only in 1916.

Denmark was in a very different position than Greece when starting the path toward a modern bureaucracy. In contrast to the modest geographical span of contemporary Denmark, Danish nobility and monarchs dominated an empire. The king controlled Greenland, Iceland, and Norway, held colonies in Africa, America, and Asia, and dominated Schleswig-Holstein. Two things are especially important to consider in this context. First, the state apparatus of Denmark was constructed to administer an empire, but by the nineteenth century Denmark had become one of the smallest states in Europe. Second, the king's control over Norway, where there were relatively few large estates, was partly what made him rank above the other landowners (Knudsen, 2006, p. 64). This control over overseas territories likely helped to bolster the king's ability to maintain his position.

Most reforms toward a meritocratic, professionalized and impersonal bureaucracy took place under absolute monarchy after 1660. Yet, several reforms prior to 1660 indicate that the Danish nobility were already positive to enacting such changes in the bureaucracy. First, the national Lutheran church would be a cornerstone in establishing the modern bureaucracy, and the role of the church in providing public services was established already prior to the absolute monarchy. For example, to improve tax collection, priests were, from 1645, required to keep "church records" with information on baptism, marriage and death, effectively implementing a system of census. Second, the education level among the Danish nobility (and other elites) was comparatively high and this trend started prior to absolutism. Especially important were sixteenth-century military reforms that reduced the role of the noble class in favor of professional mercenaries, which presumably freed up time for the Danish nobility to obtain relevant education for subsequent work in the state administration (Knudsen, 2006, pp. 56, 78).

Nevertheless, most important reforms took place after 1660. Early significant changes to the state bureaucracy pertained to improvements in the rule of law. A high court was established already in 1661 and the "Danish Laws" were published in 1682. Even the king's power as absolute was stipulated in the "Lex Regia." With the rule of law came the depersonalization of the bureaucracy; for example, a law regulating gifts to civil servants appeared in 1676. Yet, the extent of rule of law in seventeenth-century Denmark should not be exaggerated. The Danish high court faced dilemmas typical for the development of judicial independence and legitimacy and usually opted not to interfere in the king's decisions (Gøbel, 2003; Knudsen, 2006). The bureaucracy was also ridden with patrimonialism and influential individuals would often get their lackeys into positions of power. This practice was clamped down upon by the doctor of the mentally ill King Christian VII, Dr. Struensee, who acted as the de facto ruler between 1770 and 1772 (Gøbel, 2003, p. 102).

Obviously, giving a precise measure of corruption in Danish state administration at the time is difficult. Faced with this uncertainty, contemporary observers may easily judge history partly by how Denmark eventually became. One might speculate whether we would have highlighted the *impersonal* aspects of the Danish bureaucracy during the seventeenth century if the Danish state today had not been such a success. This is one reason why we strongly encourage the use of systematic measurement that enables more rigorous comparisons across countries and over time. After 1789, we have such measures from the V-Dem project. In Figure 8, we plot four important measures for Danish political development across 1789–1939. The long-dashed line is the measure of impartial and rule-following bureaucracy, the dotted line is meritocratic recruitment to the public administration, the solid line is the Polyarchy measure of democracy, and the dashed line is the share of adults with suffrage. In 1789, the year our data start, Denmark does, indeed, seem to have a very law-abiding bureaucracy, indicated by a high level of impartiality. This feature of the Danish state persisted throughout the period. The same holds true for meritocratic recruitment, except a notable reduction from the mid-1870s to the mid-1890s, before rebounding and remaining consistently high. Our measures (which are also, it should be remembered, based on the structured judgment of historical country experts) therefore largely corroborate the historical accounts that Denmark established a modern bureaucracy before the late 18th century.

Let us consider the historical development of the Danish bureaucracy toward the Weberian ideal of meritocratic recruitment more closely. Indeed, the push toward meritocratic recruitment was a significant change to Danish bureaucracy under absolutism, after 1660. The reason for this development seems connected to intra-elite competition in Danish politics. The largest threat to the king's dominance were 500–700 large landowners and it was important to Danish kings to curb the influence of these powerful individuals (Knudsen, 2006, p. 64). One main strategy was to build a bureaucracy loyal to the king by

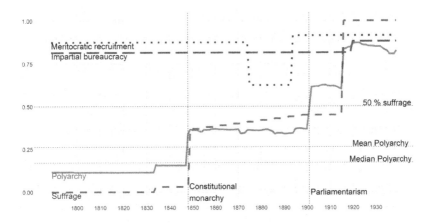

Figure 8 History of Danish institutions.

recruiting personnel among the rural freeholder farmers and urban bourgeoisie. For similar reasons, Danish kings tended to be relatively often involved in the recruitment of both civil servants and military personnel. For example, the king had to approve all loans and marriages of military personnel and, by 1770, systematic lists were compiled of all civil servants including their different skills and behavior.[5]

During absolutism, the Danish bureaucracy was likely also strengthened, indirectly, by other reform initiatives that, at first sight, seemingly had little to do with the public administration. The perhaps most famous ones enacted under the absolutist monarchy was a series of reforms in the agricultural sector in the late eighteenth century ("landboreformerne") that emancipated tenant farmers. Importantly, in 1788, the feudal law that had required peasants to remain in the estate where they were born ("stavnsbånd") was abolished. Furthermore, in the late-eighteenth century, economic hardships forced many landowners to sell plots to some of these tenants to raise capital, resulting in a (modest) redistribution of land. As more landowners could now increase their profit by adopting more efficient production methods, the agricultural sector saw rapid innovation and productivity growth at the turn of the century (Knudsen, 2006, pp. 84, 85). While the reforms were first and foremost socially important – they improved the lives of thousands of farmers – they also had positive implications for tax collection and military recruitment. Moreover, the reforms

---

[5] We note that this story could probably be presented in different ways. Had a modern African president tried to bolster his power over the opposition by recruiting a "loyal" bureaucracy, many observers might interpret this as a story of African patrimonialism. This reinforces the point on the importance of systematic measurement and comparisons.

turned the free-born farmers into an important social group in Danish society, which would play a key role in the later democratization experiences of the country.

The reforms described here coincided with a rapid expansion of the bureaucracy. In 1712, Denmark had between 66 and 80 public servants. By 1812, this number had increased to 252 (Knudsen, 2006, p. 67). As the number of decisions and size of government expanded, the Danish government also seized to be characterized by personal rule and became thoroughly "bureaucratic." The number of decisions and complexity of the system was difficult for a single individual to control. In establishing these structures, Danish kings thus undermined their own control and built the infrastructure for what would become formalized ministries with hierarchical bureaucratic structures. As Danish kings were concerned with limiting the influence of the rural landowners, they empowered freeholder farmers and the urban bourgeoisie and gave them access to government positions. These forces would eventually overthrow the king as an absolutist ruler. We cannot know if Danish kings would have instead opted to undermine the bureaucracy had they foreseen this threat. What we do know, however, is that modern Denmark is exceptional not only in terms of being a wealthy, democratic country but also for how easily it got there; many countries have suffered from rulers who were far more inclined to consolidate personal rule at the expense of development.

By the time absolutism ended in 1848, it was already severely weakened. There was no all-powerful, privileged landowning class left to defend the king. The bureaucracy was built by nonnobles and the large rural estates had lost much of their control over the rural population (Knudsen, 2006, p. 107). The final blow came from a national-liberal opposition, combined with a succession crisis in the monarchy. A constitution was adopted, a parliament erected, and suffrage was expanded to 70 percent of the male population above the age of thirty. Like in Greece, the constitution did not solve the issue of the parliamentary principle. Government ministers were still appointed by the king and there was no clear-cut solution to conflicts between parliament and government. This power struggle would not be solved until 1901.

According to our categorization of historical institutional sequences using V-Dem data, Appendix Figure B.2 shows that Denmark is categorized as a stateness-first case, with long experience of relatively impartial bureaucracy (we can only track it back to 1789) before democratization. Figure 8 shows that 1848 is the year when Denmark crosses both the median and mean value of Polyarchy in our dataset. From 1848, elections were held and suffrage was fairly inclusive, at least by standards of the day. Further, the constitutional monarchy liberalized the Danish political system in several regards. Notably, harsh censorship laws were abolished and labor rights improved, for example, with the abolishment of corporal punishment. Thus 1848 marked a significant change in the Danish political system toward a more democratic one. Regarding economic developments, taxes on land were made uniform for both small farmers and estates. Also, several market regulations were disbanded and markets liberalized.

Yet, 1848 Denmark was still a repressive system in other regards. The police was still formally allocated extensive judicial powers and it continued to enforce some censorship, limit freedom of organization, and spy on unions. Civil servants tended to be conservatives and opposition sympathizers saw their careers stagnate and sometimes lost their jobs. In Figure 8, the lines for Polyarchy have several small fluctuations in this period, corresponding to smaller changes that would affect the nature of the regime. These changes were results of different laws being implemented and used as tools in the ongoing struggle between the liberal opposition in parliament and the king and his conservative government; for example, censorship was temporarily reinstated in 1886 (Knudsen, 2006, p. 124).

The power struggle between king and parliament ended in 1901, when the conservatives faced a major electoral defeat and only got 8 out of 114 parliament seats. This was the third election in a row where the liberals became the largest party in parliament and the second election in a row where they held the majority. The king was now forced to appoint a liberal prime minister, although the parliamentary principle would not be legally codified until 1956. The developments of 1901 are reflected in Polyarchy, as the score passes the 0.5 threshold for the first time. (We apply this stricter threshold in some of our robustness tests on the stateness-first thesis below). With universal suffrage in 1916, Polyarchy increases once more to about 0.8.

By 1901, the core bureaucratic structures of the modern Danish state had long been established. However, we highlight that democratic Denmark also embarked on several important reforms. For example, the tax system remained structured around property at the turn of century and a modern income tax was not adopted until in 1904. Furthermore, the liberal government, whose voters came from families of the many peasants liberated from the estates 100 years earlier, decentralized government and democratized local politics. Judicial independence and the separation of powers was reformed in 1919 (Knudsen, 2006, pp. 151, 152). These developments are also reflected in our measure of impartial and rule-following bureaucracy, which increases somewhat after the 1919 reforms. In sum, several reforms, taking Denmark even further toward an impersonal and professionalized bureaucracy, occurred after the country democratized.

Nineteenth- and early twentieth-century Denmark was not only a success story in terms of democratization and (maintenance and some further expansion of) state capacity, it was also an economic success story. We will not go into details on the economic policies and development of the Danish economy, other than note that GDP per capita growth was comparatively high and fairly consistent during this era, especially after 1848. According to the Maddison data, Danish GDP per capita was 1,706 USD (2011 prices) in 1820 and 2,160 USD in 1848, giving an annual GDP per capita growth rate of 0.8 percent. Between 1848 and 1901, GDP per capita grew at an annual rate of 1.4 percent and from 1901 to 1939 it grew at 1.5 percent. At the eve of WWII, Denmark's GDP per capita stood at 7,832 USD. This compared favorably not only to Greece (3,620 USD in 1939) but also countries such as France (6,058 USD) and The Netherlands (6,006 USD). The Danish economy has continued to prosper since then and the question that we ask is this: Does this strong and consistent record of economic development stem from the fact that Denmark, under absolutist rule, built a capable state before democracy was introduced?

5.2.1 Synthetic Control

We repeat the same synthetic control procedure that we did for Greece, for Denmark. This time, the question that we want to answer is: Did the stateness-first sequence of institutional change observed in Denmark contribute to its (rapid) economic development? Our synthetic control, "Denmark," is first modeled to mimic Denmark by drawing on countries that did *not* experience democratization during the same time period (around 1848) but were otherwise fairly similar to Denmark in relevant regards. Corroborating evidence for the stateness-first argument, would be that economic growth increases more in Denmark relative to in "Denmark," after Denmark democratizes.

Following our benchmark median-threshold rule, the 1848 regime change counts as the first instance of democratization in Denmark. Once again, we draw on information from four variables – ln GDP p.c., impartial and rule-following bureaucracy, ethnic heterogeneity, and geographical region – to construct the synthetic control, "Denmark." This fictive country is composed by drawing on the characteristics of three countries: Saudi Arabia/Nejd, Russia, and Japan. The two first countries have the most impact on the predicted values, respectively 49 percent and 47 percent, while Japan accounts for approximately 3 percent.

We highlight right away that the match here is far worse than it was for Greece. Notably, "Denmark" has much lower bureaucratic capacity than the real Denmark. The problem is that there are simply no countries that are similar

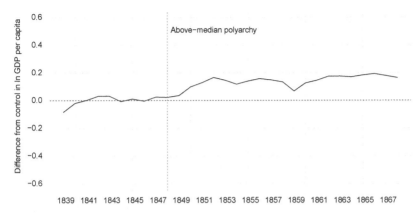

Figure 9 The difference in ln GDP p.c. between Denmark and "Denmark" from 10 years before to 20 years after democratization.

to Denmark and that do not experience democratization during the relevant time period (1839–68). For the sake of consistency with the analysis of Greece, we show the results but offer alternative and probably better, specifications.

The results for this first specification are illustrated in Figure 9. After democratization, Denmark does, indeed, have consistently higher economic growth compared to "Denmark" across the twenty-year period after democratization. This observation stands in contrast to the results for Greece, where democratization was not as beneficial for economic growth, at least in the short term after the transition. So far then, we have some evidence to support the stateness-first argument.

Due to the poor match, however, we do not put much faith in these results. Instead, we repeat the same synthetic control procedure but remove the restriction that the matching countries need to be from the same thirty-year period (1839–68), just like we did for Greece. With this approach, "Denmark" is constructed as a mix of The Netherlands 1819–48 (68 percent) and Austria 1818–47 (32 percent). In addition to being located in Europe, these countries are much more similar to Denmark in terms of their bureaucratic capacity. We therefore believe this second version of "Denmark" is a far better comparison to Denmark, despite drawing on information from slightly different time periods. The results from this second analysis are illustrated in Figure 10. The beneficial effect of democratization in Denmark is still present, albeit far from as strong and consistent across the period. This latter analysis thus only provides fairly weak evidence in support of the stateness-first argument.

To summarise, our results so far do not offer strong support or grounds for falsification of the stateness-first argument. We hesitate to draw any strong

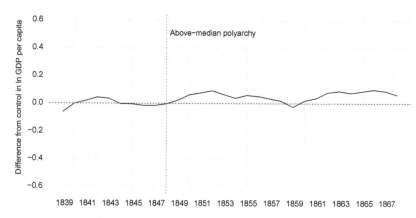

Figure 10 The difference in ln GDP p.c. between Denmark and "Denmark" from 10 years before to 20 years after democratization, allowing the countries in the synthetic control to be from other 30 year periods than 1839–68.

conclusions from results presented so far. For instance, we found some support for the argument from our synthetic control analysis of the Danish case but not from the Greek case. We hope, however, that the brief case studies of Denmark and Greece have illustrated three important points pertaining to analysis of institutional sequencing and its effects.

First, Denmark and Greece are poorly fit for direct comparisons and qualitative historical evidence stemming from direct comparisons of such cases is a risky endeavor. These countries' histories diverge in far more ways than their sequence of institutional adoption. Furthermore, for both countries, it is difficult to find other cases that are clearly suitable comparisons. We surmise that these points would hold true for most other cases typically invoked as providing evidence for the stateness-first argument in the literature. Inference comes with several trade-offs, such as trading away strict similarity in temporal similarity for similarity on the variables of interest. There are no perfect strategies.

Second, determining exactly when a bureaucracy turned sufficiently sophisticated or when a country is sufficiently democratic, is riddled with ambiguity. This is an essential problem for the stateness-first argument, which implies clear categorical differences on theoretical concepts that are best understood as continuous and, as argued by Mazzuca and Munck (2014), often evolved in tandem. We were able to structure the discussion on measurement and institutional development by using historical data from V-Dem. Most existing historical accounts discussing the stateness-first argument have not had this benefit, thereby further exacerbating the issues of measurement uncertainty (and possibly resulting biases).

Third, developments in countries such as Greece and Denmark may be affected by a number of "random factors" not incorporated in our parsimonious model and therefore may not be generalizable. In fact, we consider the issue of case selection (of a handful of cases) to be one of the main obstacles for drawing valid, general inferences in the stateness-first literature. To more appropriately scrutinize the general stateness-first hypothesis, we need to systematically draw on information from a much larger set of countries.

5.3 Synthetic Control Studies: Global Sample

For the reasons just discussed, we repeated the synthetic control procedures used for Greece and Denmark for the first democratization episode (i.e., moving across the median Polyarchy threshold) of all countries where we could construct an appropriate synthetic control with available data. As with Denmark and Greece, we control for the geographic region and ethnic composition of the country, in addition to bureaucratic capacity and ln GDP per capita (p.c.). We are not able to produce a synthetic control for all countries in the world. This is not an artifact of the method but rather a feature of world history; some countries are simply so unique that it is difficult to find proper comparisons. Whenever there is too much difference between the country and its synthetic control in the GDP p.c. trend prior to democratization, this also indicates that a constructed synthetic control may not constitute a proper counterfactual after all. We therefore removed all countries that had a difference of more than 0.2 divergence (in ln GDP p.c.) from its synthetic control at any point in the pre-democratization period. In the end, this left us with thirty-seven countries in the group that democratized at relatively low state capacity (below the median threshold on impartial administration) and thirty democratizers in the high-capacity group. The countries and the composition of their synthetic controls are listed in Appendix Tables B.2 and B.3.

The leftmost plot of Figure 11 illustrates the difference between a country's ln GDP p.c. and its synthetic control's (one grey line per country), for countries with below-median values on impartial bureaucracy at its first episode of democratization (i.e., democracy-first countries). The black line represents the local average (loess line, with 95 percent confidence intervals) for all country-lines. The rightmost plot repeats the procedure for all countries with available synthetic controls and above-median values on impartial bureaucracy at the first episode of democratization (i.e., stateness-first countries). Two implications of (certain formulations of) the stateness-first

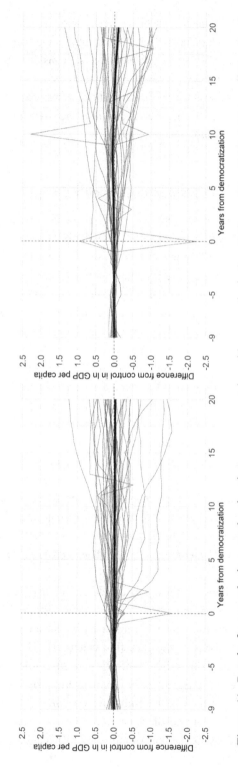

Figure 11 Results from synthetic control estimation among countries with, respectively, low (left panel) and high (right panel) levels of bureaucratic impartiality. Democratization is here defined as the first year the country had an above-median value on *Polyarchy*. Each gray line indicates the difference in ln GDP p.c. (y-axis) per year (x-axis) for one specific country compared to that country's synthetic control. The thick black line and gray ribbon indicates the local average (loess) and its 95% confidence interval across all the individual estimations.

argument are that democratization in low-capacity states should be detrimental to economic growth, whereas democratization in high-capacity states should enhance subsequent growth. There is no evidence of such a pattern in the data. Democratization simply does not seem to have any *systematic* effect on economic growth in either scenario.

We contend that the juxtaposition of this broad analysis with results from (especially) the analysis of Denmark serves to illustrates how the selection of cases to study easily can shape results and more general conclusions. Cases are sometimes, inadvertently or consciously, cherry-picked: Denmark and Greece may be chosen based on researchers a priori knowledge of how they behave both on the dependent *and* independent variable and therefore these cases are likely to correspond well to the theory underlying the stateness-first argument. We therefore put much more faith in the general analysis than in the analysis of these two countries, viewed in isolation.

Just like we did with Greece and Denmark, we conducted additional tests where we relaxed the requirement that countries used for the synthetic controls have to be from the same thirty-year time period. Hopefully, this increases the overall substantive similarity between the treatment countries and synthetic controls, at the expense of temporal similarity. These results are presented in Figure 12. Once again, the leftmost plot illustrates the difference between a country's ln GDP p.c. and its synthetic control's ln GDP p.c. for democracy-first countries. Details on these analyses can be found in the Appendix Tables B.4 and B.5. The rightmost plot repeats the procedure for all stateness-first countries. Democratization, on average, enhances economic growth in both the medium-term in democracy-first and stateness-first scenarios in this particular specification. Hence, even though the point estimates are slightly higher, on average, for the stateness-first group, these results do not give strong corroboration of the stateness-first argument either.

In sum, we find mixed results on implications from the stateness-first argument so far. Neither the case studies of Greece and Denmark gave any clear support to the stateness-first argument (although the evidence was somewhat more in line with the argument for Denmark) and the synthetic control analysis of sixty-seven countries even opened up the possibility for a general, unconditional net *benefit* of democratization. However, our analyses provide no final verdict. The synthetic control method is just one of many possible ways to empirically investigate the stateness-first argument. In the next section, we will test assumptions behind and several implications from the stateness-first argument, outlined in Section 3.1, by using different statistical approaches.

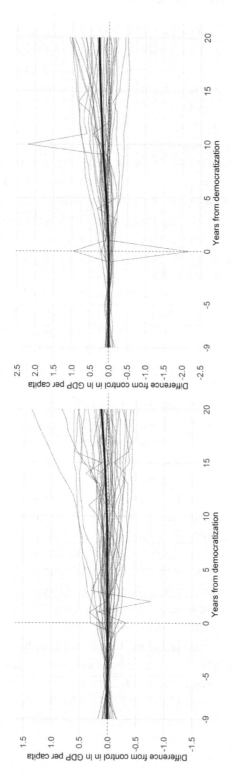

Figure 12 Results from synthetic control estimation among countries with, respectively, low (left panel) and high (right panel) levels of bureaucratic impartiality. Democratization is here defined as the first year the country had an above-median value on *Polyarchy*. Each gray line indicates the difference in ln GDP p.c. (*y*-axis) per year (*x*-axis) for one specific country compared to that country's synthetic control. The thick black line and gray ribbon indicates the local average (loess) and its 95% confidence interval across all the individual estimations. The countries donating to the synthetic control do not have to be from the same 30-year time period as the respective treatment country.

6 Testing the Stateness-First Argument

In this section, we gauge the validity of the stateness-first argument by using three different approaches to testing, namely panel regression, non-parametric matching, and sequence analysis.

Our dependent variables draw on the extensive real Gross Domestic Product per capita (GDP p.c.) data from Fariss et al. (2017), which allow us to extend the analysis back to 1789 and include about 180 polities in the most extensive samples. To mitigate measurement error, which is present in all existing measures of GDP (Jerven, 2013), Fariss et al. employed a dynamic latent trait model to produce less error-prone estimates from several GDP (and population) sources. We use their point estimates benchmarked in the Maddison time series. In addition to mitigating different types of measurement error, Fariss et al.'s routine for imputation of missing values helps reduce sample selection biases (Honaker and King, 2010). We conduct robustness tests by using the updated version (by Bolt and van Zanden, curated via V-Dem) of the original GDP series from Maddison. We then interpolate GDP p.c. between observations (often every tenth year in the nineteenth century), by assuming constant growth rates in these intervals.

We employ both forward-lagged ln GDP p.c. (controlling for initial ln GDP p.c.) and average annual GDP p.c. growth, across different time intervals, as dependent variables. The former dependent variable measures income level and the latter measures rate of economic growth. While both approaches, in practice, allow us to estimate the effect of institutions and institutional sequences on average growth across the specified time period (for a discussion on the characteristics and mathematical similarities of these approaches, see, e.g., Hoeffler, 2002), the two specifications have some econometric differences. The approach using GDP p.c. growth directly as dependent variable allows us to better model conditional convergence mechanisms (see Barro and Sala-i Martin, 2004), whereas the approach using forward lagged (logged) GDP p.c. level as dependent variable is less sensitive to measurement errors in GDP p.c. and gives regressions with higher explained variance (R-squared).

Countries' GDP p.c. time series is characterized by strong serial correlation and there may be presence of a unit root in autoregressive models where GDP p.c. is the dependent variable. This can create different problems when trying to identify the relationship between state capacity, democracy and income, especially when using standard OLS models. Notably, causally unrelated time trends in these three measures could bias regression coefficients. We try out different strategies for mitigating these concerns. We always cluster standard errors to account for panel-specific serial correlation, and we also test models using GDP p.c. growth as the dependent variable instead of ln GDP per capita (which is basically equivalent to first-differencing the dependent variable). Further, we conduct AR-tests to check for residual autocorrelation and add extra lags on the dependent variable in some specifications. Moreover, both the CEM models and the already-presented synthetic controls are less sensitive to such time trends. Hence, we find it plausible that our results are not an artefact of serial correlation or unit root problems.

Before we proceed to present the different statistical specifications and results, let us provide a quick road map of the types of tests (of different assumptions and implications of the stateness-first argument) contained in the section.

First, we run panel regressions. With this approach, we mainly consider a key assumption undergirding the stateness-first argument, namely that democracy produces better outcomes – here higher economic growth – in high-capacity than in low-capacity states. We run panel regressions on split samples, according to regime type, and we also run interaction specifications to see if the effect of democracy on growth varies systematically with level of state capacity. These tests include a large number of observations and are thus very efficient. They also allow for quite conservative control strategies, including the control for country- and time-fixed effects, to isolate the effects of particular institutional features. We also use panel regressions to test an implication of the stateness-first argument by assessing how level of state capacity before or at the time of a democratization event affects subsequent economic growth.

Second, we present regression models estimated after pre-parametric coarsened exact matching where the matching procedures embed different assumptions about the proper counterfactual comparisons made under the stateness-first argument. Most of these tests do allow for cross-country variation to inform results, as is, indeed, the approach also in the more qualitative and case-study oriented literature supporting the stateness-first argument. While this opens up for omitted, country-specific factors influencing results, one benefit of the approach is the strict focus on comparisons of otherwise similar countries (thus resembling the synthetic control approach in Section 5).

Third, we perform sequence analysis, which arguably provides the most appropriate test of the stateness-first argument's main empirical implication. In these tests, we link economic growth to the historical *sequence* of institutional adoption that is proposed as beneficial in the stateness-first argument and contrast with alternative sequences, notably the democracy-first sequence. With this approach, we are also capable of isolating historical sequences of institutional change from "levels" (current or historical) of either state capacity or democracy as well as the accumulated time during which a country has been democratic or a high-capacity state.

To quickly summarize our findings: Neither of these three approaches to testing uncover any clear evidence consistent with the stateness-first argument.

6.1 Panel Regressions

We start by running an ordinary least squares (OLS) specification with country-year as unit of analysis and errors clustered by country. The clustering of errors is done to account for autocorrelation within the panel-units (countries). Our benchmark model controls for lagged ln GDP p.c. alongside country- and year-fixed effects. The year-fixed effects help account for (non-linear) time trends and shorter-term global shocks to economic growth and institutional features, insofar as these trends and shocks are common to all units. Trends in global growth patterns could, for example, be driven by differential rates of technological change throughout modern history and global shocks could be due to, for example, global financial crises, world wars, or pandemics. The country-fixed effects address country-specific, time-invariant factors related to geography, culture, etc., that may simultaneously affect institutional and economic development. The ability to control for such hard-to-observe confounders is a distinct advantage of the panel models, both relative to existing studies that draw on historical country narratives and to large-N studies (including models in the next section) that draw on cross-country comparisons. As noted Section 5, countries such as Greece and Denmark could experience differential rates of economic growth for a variety of reasons that are specific to each country and which may be hard to measure properly.

We intentionally keep our benchmark parsimonious to mitigate so-called "posttreatment biases"; democracy and state capacity may influence variables such as civil war or natural resource dependence, which, in turn, affects economic growth. If we control for such "intermediate variables" that are placed between institutional adoption and economic growth in the causal chain, we will eliminate relevant indirect effects that we want to capture. We want to assess the "total effect" of institutions on economic growth, also when this effect is partly channeled via, say, enhancing the risk of civil war. We do include natural resource dependence, civil war and other controls in subsequent tests that prioritize mitigating omitted variable bias over posttreatment bias. Although, say, civil war may be affected by the institutional environment, it may also affect regime change and level of state capacity. The extra models controlling for civil war (and other variables) help us guard against the latter scenario driving out results.

The time horizon of the institutional effects proposed by (different) stateness-first argument(s) are not well specified in the previous literature and one might expect both shorter- and longer-term effects. Therefore, we try out different time lag specifications. We begin by measuring the outcome twenty years after the covariates to gauge the medium-term effects of democracy in contexts of high and low state capacity.

We first employ ln GDP p.c measured in $t + 20$ as the outcome and run our benchmark on subsamples of low-capacity (Model 1, Table 1) and high-capacity (Model 2) states. In addition to the control variables – initial level (in year t) of ln GDP p.c. and country- and year-fixed effects – we include our main measure of electoral democracy, V-Dem's Polyarchy index, as a covariate. To produce balanced subsamples of relatively low- and high-capacity states, we split by the median sample value (-0.286) on our main measure of state capacity, V-Dem's impartial and rule-following administration indicator.

As displayed in the leftmost columns of Table 1, Polyarchy has a negative coefficient in the low-capacity sample (Model 1) and a positive coefficient in the high-capacity sample (Model 2). The point estimates thereby indicate that democracy may be detrimental to growth in low-capacity contexts and bene-ficial to growth in high-capacity contexts. Yet, we cannot conclude on these patterns, as the uncertainty surrounding the point estimates is substantial rela-tive to the estimated sizes of the effects. Indeed, the Polyarchy coefficients are indistinguishable from zero – or statistically insignificant – at conventional lev-els in both subsamples. Results are similar when we replace ln GDP p.c. level with average annual GDP p.c. growth over the twenty-year period as dependent variable. These results are displayed in Models 3 (low capacity) and 4 (high capacity).[6] The Appendix reports several additional specifications, including regressions on alternatively specified subsamples. Split-sample specifications using very high/low thresholds for the high-/low-capacity samples do not show any clear evidence supporting the stateness-first argument either.

Yet, one may remark that we are not primarily interested in assessing the effect of democracy in low- and high-capacity samples separately – although several contributions making stateness-first arguments do, indeed, hypothesize such relationships – but rather in assessing whether or not the effect of democ-racy on growth systematically changes as state capacity increases. To properly evaluate such a relationship, we turn to interaction specifications. More specif-ically, Model 5 in Table 1 is our benchmark interaction specification run on the

---

[6] As expected, the ln GDP p.c. coefficient flips sign. Higher initial income predicts higher subse-quent income but slower subsequent growth rates, as anticipated by the conditional convergence argument.

	(1)	(2)	(3)	(4)	(5)	(6)	(7)	(8)	(9)	(10)	(11)
Sample	LC	HC	LC	HC	Full	Full	Full	Full	Full	Full	Full
Estimator	OLS	OLS	OLS	OLS	OLS	OLS	OLS	OLS	OLS	GMM	GMM
Panel length	1 yr	1 yr	1 yr	1 yr	1 yr	1 yr	1 yr	1 yr	1 yr	10 yrs	10 yrs
Dep var (level/growth)	Level	Level	Growth	Growth	Level	Growth	Level	Level	Level	Level	Level
Dep var measured in year	$t + 20$	$t + 20$	t to $t + 20$	t to $t + 20$	$t + 20$	t to $t + 20$	$t + 20$	$t + 20$	$t + 40$	$t + 20$	$t + 10$
	b/(se)	b/(se)	b/(se)	b/(se)	b/(se)	b/(se)	b/(se)	b/(se)	b/(se)	b/(se)	b/(se)
Polyarchy	−0.146	0.169	−0.705	0.742	−0.095	−0.518		−0.145	−0.044	0.294	0.284*
	(0.189)	(0.119)	(0.963)	(0.593)	(0.121)	(0.610)		(0.121)	(0.192)	(0.269)	(0.133)
Polyarchy X Impartial adm.					0.081	0.436		0.043	0.099	−0.109	−0.116*
					(0.048)	(0.248)		(0.040)	(0.092)	(0.087)	(0.049)
BMR democracy							−0.012				
							(0.039)				
BMR X Impartial adm.							0.008				
							(0.021)				
Impartial adm.					0.011	0.044	0.018	0.022	−0.004	0.056	0.070**
					(0.019)	(0.094)	(0.019)	(0.022)	(0.034)	(0.033)	(0.026)
Civil war								−0.024			
								(0.040)			
Resource dependence								−0.007**			
								(0.002)			
Ln Population								0.001			
								(0.046)			
Ln GDP pc (in t)	0.858**	0.631**	−0.738**	−1.873**	0.786**	−1.098**	0.799**	0.793**	0.665**	1.033**	0.970**
	(0.051)	(0.064)	(0.266)	(0.328)	(0.047)	(0.239)	(0.042)	(0.043)	(0.073)	(0.077)	(0.039)
Country dummies	Y	Y	Y	Y	Y	Y	Y	Y	Y	Y	Y
Year/period dummies	Y	Y	Y	Y	Y	Y	Y	Y	Y	Y	Y
N	8,032	8,056	8,079	8,165	16,080	16,236	12,644	10,819	12,749	1,676	1,863
Countries	132	151	133	151	183	184	180	160	162	176	186
Maximum years/periods	206	206	202	206	206	206	195	179	186	21	22
R^2	0.751	0.893	0.303	0.409	0.838	0.327	0.856	0.852	0.771		
Number of instruments										169	178
Hansen J-test p-value										0.891	0.895
AR(2) test p-value										0.150	0.745

Notes: $* p < 0.05$; $** p < 0.01$. Constant, country, and year dummies omitted. Errors clustered by country in OLS and robust in (System) GMM. LC: Low capacity. HC: High capacity, determined relative to median-sample value on IPA (−0.286) for full sample for specification corresponding to Models 1 and 2.

full sample with ln GDP p.c. as dependent variable. This model, which draws on 16,080 country-year observations from 183 countries, simultaneously includes Polyarchy, impartial and rule-following administration and a multiplicative interaction term (Polyarchy X impartial administration). The estimated relationship between democracy and growth does, indeed, increase in state capacity but, once again, the interaction pattern is not statistically significant at the conventional 5 percent level. However, we note that the interaction coefficient is weakly significant with a t-value of 1.68. Also, in Model 6, which uses GDP p.c. growth as outcome, the interaction coefficient is statistically significant at the 10 percent level but not the 5 percent level.

However, we immediately remark that findings in favor of a positive interaction between democracy and state capacity are even weaker in alternative model specifications. There is no evidence of any systematic interaction pattern in Model 7, which substitutes Polyarchy with the dichotomous BMR measure, nor in Model 8, which returns to the benchmark using the Polyarchy regime measure but controls for population (Fariss et al., 2017), natural resources income/GDP (Miller, 2015) and civil war (Haber and Menaldo, 2011). In general, the (null) result is fairly consistent across sets of plausible controls and when focusing on suffrage rather than broader democracy measures (see Appendix C).

Regarding the time frame for the dependent variable, the 20-year lag period is admittedly arbitrary but aims to balance different concerns by choosing an intermediate time interval. Longer lags help ensure that we pick up additional longer-term effects, if they exist, but also allow for additional "random events" in the intervening years to add noise. Further tests show nonrobust results for both shorter and longer time frames. Model 9 illustrates the latter, measuring ln GDP p.c. in $t + 40$. Figure 13 displays interaction coefficients from versions of Model 6 (on average annual GDP p.c. growth), with varying time-period length from five to fifty years for measuring growth. The indications of an interactive relationship in line with the stateness-first argument are somewhat stronger when considering growth in the shorter term (see also Appendix C). Yet, results are not clear and robust even for these shorter time lags. In sum, there is no strong support, so far, for the core assumption of the stateness-first argument that democracy is more conducive to development in high-capacity than in low-capacity contexts.

We also employed the system Generalized Method of Moments (GMM) estimator, which is appropriate for dealing with slow-moving variables such as democracy and state capacity (Blundell and Bond, 1998). Importantly, GMM allows us to treat democracy and state capacity as endogenous regressors. Model 10, which measures ln GDP p.c. in $t + 20$, displays a negative but

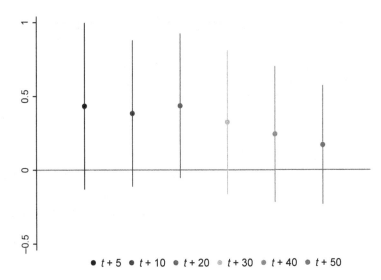

Figure 13 Coefficients with 95% confidence intervals for multiplicative interaction term between Polyarchy and Impartial Public Administration. Specifications resemble Model 6, Table 1, with average annual GDP p.c. growth as outcome but the length of the time period for which the outcomes is measured varies.

insignificant interaction term, and Model 11 a negative and statistically significant one (at 5 percent). The relevant specification tests of the model (AR(2)- and Hansen J-tests) suggest that this latter model gives consistent estimates. Hence, Model 11 indicates that democracy actually has a more benevolent medium-term effect on growth in lower-capacity states. One possible reason for why the GMM results differ from the (insignificant) OLS results relates to the former modeling the institutional features as endogenous rather than exogenous. The OLS specifications may, to take one hypothetical example, underestimate the effect of democracy on growth in low-capacity settings, since they fail to incorporate that both democratization and slow posttransition growth might follow the start of severe (pre-transition) economic crises. Several alternative GMM specifications replicate the negative and significant interaction, suggesting that democracy enhances growth more in low-capacity settings. Yet, the significance of the result is not robust, for example, to the number of lagged dependent variables included as regressors (Appendix Table C.5).

We ran numerous additional tests on the benchmark OLS specifications – both interaction and split-sample tests – using different measures of democracy, state capacity, and GDP p.c. to check sensitivity. Most results are reported in Appendix C. First, the null results are retained when using alternative democracy measures, including V-Dem's suffrage measure. Second, results are very similar when using the Maddison GDP data instead of the Fariss et al. (2017) estimates (presented in Appendix Table C.4). Third, results mostly hold up for different measures of state capacity. Appendix Figure C.1 shows split-sample tests akin to the benchmark from Table 1, but using median scores on alternative measures of bureaucracy features from V-Dem v.10, namely meritocratic recruitment and remuneration of bureaucrats well as latent measures of state capacity (from Hanson and Sigman, 2019) and information capacity (from Brambor et al., 2019). For V-Dem's remuneration of officials and Brambor et al.'s information capacity measures, we find a larger, positive effect of democracy on growth in high-capacity states. We find no systematic difference for the other measures. The results from this latter exercise are quite similar when we substitute Polyarchy with the dichotomous BMR measure, as revealed in Appendix Figure C.2. This time, we only find indications of a stronger, positive relationship between democracy and growth in the high-capacity sample when using the bureaucratic remuneration/salaried officials variable from V-Dem but not when using V-Dem's measure of meritocratic recruitment, the latent measure of state capacity from Hanson and Sigman (2019), or the latent measure of information capacity from Brambor et al. (2019). The overall conclusion must be that the pattern of (mainly) null-results holds up to different combinations of measures of democracy and state capacity.

Another test of the stateness-first argument is to assess changes in growth rates from before to after recorded democratization episodes and check whether posttransition increases in growth are more likely after democratization in high-capacity states.[7] The Appendix discusses such panel regressions, for instance using BMR to identify democratization episodes. These tests do not corroborate the stateness-first argument. This is illustrated by Figure 14, which contains four scatter plots that map the difference between the posttransition growth rate, measured as average annual growth over the twenty years after transition and the pre-transition growth rate, measured for the twenty years before transition. This difference in growth rates is mapped along the y-axes, with ten-year pre-transition averages on four proxies of state capacity along the x-axes. In addition to the impartial and rule-following administration measure, we use V-Dem measures on corruption, clientelism, and meritocratic recruitment. Overall, there is substantial variation in posttransition growth changes, both among low- and high-capacity states. Several countries grow faster after a democratization episode but others do not. The best-fit lines and confidence intervals reveal no systematic and robust patterns, although for

---

[7] Specifically, the causal effect defined in Equation 1 in Section 3.1.

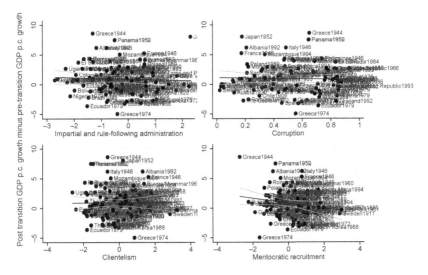

Figure 14 Proxies of state capacity and change in growth rate from before to after transition on BMR democracy measure. Notes: Average 20-years posttransition GDP p.c. growth minus average 20-years pretransition GDP p.c. growth along the y-axis and 10-year average pretransition scores on rule-following bureaucracy (upper-left), corruption (upper-right), clientelism (lower-left) and meritocratic recruitment (lower-right; data from V-Dem v.10) along x-axes. The scatterplots are overlaid with best-fit lines and 95% confidence intervals.

the meritocratic recruitment measure there is a discernible pattern of larger average increases in postdemocratization growth for countries transitioning at low capacity. This observed pattern conflicts with the stateness-first argument, which predicts a greater growth-benefit from democratization in high-capacity contexts.

Overall, most panel specifications and cross-section models on episodes of democratic transition suggest that there is no difference in the relationship between democratization and growth in high-capacity and low-capacity states. Hence, these tests are not supportive of the stateness-first argument. We turn to alternative tests to further evaluate this and other empirical implications of the argument.

6.2 Matching Analysis

Panel regressions, as those run in the previous section, have several advantages. Yet, they also draw on information and comparisons from across a (large) sample of quite different observations. In this section, we employ matching methods and attempt to draw information only from comparisons of relatively similar observations, which we use to construct plausible counterfactual scenarios of different kinds. More specifically, matching models allow us to draw inferences from (only) comparing otherwise similar units that differ on the treatment variable, and we use these models to assess both medium- and longer-term development effects. In Section 3.1, we discussed how it is unclear what the most appropriate counterfactual comparisons actually are when evaluating the stateness-first argument. The choice of contrast class depends on specific assumptions concerning, for instance, how democracy influences state building. To reflect different such considerations, we present tests making different assumptions about appropriate counterfactuals and we mainly employ coarsened exact matching (CEM) models (see Iacus et al., 2012).

Our first matching designs resemble the logic of the panel specifications. We herein compare countries that experienced democratization with autocratic countries, but only allow for comparisons within groups of otherwise similar countries. In this analysis, we do not find that a rule-following and impartial bureaucracy at the time of democratization enhances subsequent economic development. Subsequent matching models, which restrict the focus to the first instance of democratization in a country's history, also show no evidence that impartial and rule-following bureaucracy at democratization is related to contemporary economic performance. Further, we only compare countries that underwent democratization experiences but did so under contexts of relatively high and low state capacity. We find no support for the hypothesis that transitioning under high capacity corresponds with higher subsequent economic development.

All models include the following matching variables: year of democratization, GDP p.c. at democratization, and – since this set-up cannot account for country-fixed effects – geographic region and ethnic fractionalization score (from Alesina et al., 2003). CEM demands that all variables are categorized for the matching, and observations are only compared with observations placed in the exact same categories. Hence, there is a trade-off between only comparing very similar observations (fine-grained categories) and having many observations with available matches (broader categories). In some models, we group the year of democratization variable into three categories, with cut-offs chosen to reflect various "waves of democratization" (Huntington 1991). In others, we compare on exact year of democratization. Ln GDP p.c. is always recoded into three categories ($<$ 1st quartile; 1st–3rd quartiles; $>$ 3rd quartile). Ethnic fractionalization and the rule-following and impartial bureaucracy measures are recast into binary variables, with median values as thresholds. We always run (OLS) regressions post-matching to account for differences on covariates also within the categories. When doing so, we use the continuous versions of these variables as covariates.[8] Once again, we operationalize "democratization" as going from below to above the median on Polyarchy in our benchmark.

As noted, in our first matching designs we compare countries that experienced democratization with autocratic countries – that is, the treatment that we match on is democratization – but only allow for comparisons (within groups) of countries that are otherwise similar, following the rules outlined and matching on democratization year. Thus, we only compare countries with below-median scores on the rule-following and impartial public administration measure with each other and similarly for above-median countries. Then, in the regressions, we estimate whether scores on the impartial and rule-following administration measure *at the time of democratization* systematically predict differences in logged income twenty years later. This is an approximation of Equation 1 in Section 3.1. The fairly long time lag should allow us to pick up a development-enhancing effect of bureaucratic capacity at democratization *if* such an effect exists.[9] Initially, we allow countries to enter with more than one democratization episode, but to avoid mixing effects from multiple episodes we only include democratization episodes that follow twenty years of consecutive autocratic rule.

The results from this CEM specification are reported in Model 1, Table 2. The coefficient on impartial and rule-following administration is negative, very small (-0.06) and far from significant ($t = 0.7$). Hence, we do not find that a rule-following and impartial bureaucracy *at the time of democratization* enhances subsequent economic development.

Since our democratization measure is constructed by a cut-off on a continuous scale, one worry is that some countries could tip just above median-Polyarchy one year and then revert back into the autocracy category the next year, for example, due to measurement error. Therefore, we re-estimated Model 1 by restricting the definition of democratization to situations when a country passed the median-threshold and stayed above it for ten consecutive years. The downside to using this "ten-year rule" is that it introduces a form of posttreatment bias; democracies with higher growth are more likely avoid democratic regressions (Kennedy, 2010; Przeworski and Limongi, 1997) and

---

[8] CEM groups similar observations into subclasses and weights the observations based on the ratio of treatment/control observations. We use these weights in all regressions, which also include subclass-fixed effects.

[9] Yet, the long time lag may attenuate effects if the autocracies that we compare our "democratizers" with experience democratization in between when our independent and dependent variables are measured. We account for this issue in additional tests by omitting such observations and we test different lag lengths in the Appendix.

Table 2 CEM Balancing

	(1) Ln GDP p.c. 20 years after democratization	(2) Ln GDP p.c. in 2004	(3) Ln GDP p.c. 20 years after democratization	(4) Ln GDP p.c. in 2004	(5) Ln GDP p.c. in 2004
Bureaucracy level at democratization	−0.02	0.02	0.04	0.01	0.11
	(0.03)	(0.05)	(0.04)	(0.08)	(0.11)
Ln GDP p.c. at democratization	0.77**	0.69**	0.27	0.84**	0.60
	(0.09)	(0.10)	(0.19)	(0.27)	(0.47)
Ln year at democratization	−35.37	73.35	0.32	0.01	−9.17
	(74.20)	(156.31)	(5.28)	(10.55)	(12.94)
Ethnic fractionalization at democratization	−0.29	−0.02	0.22	−0.04	0.25
	(0.26)	(0.35)	(0.51)	(0.92)	(1.75)
Constant	268.42	−551.97	2.71	2.55	73.91
	(559.44)	(1,183.14)	(40.24)	(80.16)	(98.43)
Regional dummies	Yes	Yes	Yes	Yes	Yes
Subclass dummies	Yes	Yes	Yes	Yes	Yes
Comparison:	Demo. vs Aut.	Demo. vs Aut.	Democratizers	Democratizers	Democratizers
Democratization rule:	After 20 years of Aut.	First only	First only	First only	First only
Observations	235	312	62	71	22
R^2	0.90	0.90	0.72	0.84	0.94
Adjusted R^2	0.86	0.87	0.63	0.77	0.89

Notes: * $p < 0.05$; ** $p < 0.01$; Standard error in parentheses.

democratic regression and wider political instability is one mechanism, proposed in stateness-first accounts, through which transitions under low capacity could mitigate growth. However, the insignificant impartial and rule-following administration coefficient barely changes when employing the ten-year rule (Appendix Table C.6). Results are also fairly stable to using alternative thresholds on Polyarchy, the dichotomous BMR measure of electoral democracy, or a dummy registering if 50 percent of the adult population is enfranchised, although one specification using the 0.5 cutoff for democracy and one specification using the mean-value cutoff lends support to the stateness-first argument (see Appendix section C).

Yet, twenty years might not capture *longer-term* differences in development coming from experiencing democratization at different levels of state capacity, and several stateness-first accounts focus on developmental consequences in the very long run. Hence, the outcome variable in Model 2, Table 2, is ln GDP p.c. measured in 2004, which is the year with the best data coverage after 2000. In this specification, we only use the *first* democratization episode recorded in a country's history. This is consistent with the notion that political instability and democratic deterioration are partly consequences of the first democratic transition happening under conditions of weak state capacity. Thus, even if subsequent transitions carry an effect on economic development, these effects may be viewed as indirect effects of the first historical transition and, if so, should not be controlled for. We match countries that experienced their first democratization with an autocratic country observed in the same year and otherwise follow the matching procedure outlined previously. Model 2 shows no evidence that impartial and rule-following bureaucracy at democratization is related to contemporary economic performance. The relationship is weak (0.02) and statistically insignificant at conventional levels.

Employing a different set of comparisons, the last three models in Table 2 *only* compare countries that underwent democratization experiences, but which did so under contexts of relatively high and low state capacity. This is the descriptive argument defined in Equation 2 in Section 3.1. Hence, the treatment that we match on is the dichotomized measure of impartial and rule-following bureaucracy. Otherwise, we follow the template from before. Model 3 measures the outcome twenty years after democratization, whereas Model 4 measures the outcome in 2004. We find no support for the hypothesis that transitioning under high-capacity states corresponds with higher subsequent economic development, be it in the medium or longer term.

In Model 5, we compare countries that are about equally democratic and have about equally capable bureaucracies today, but which have different institutional-sequencing histories. First, we subset the data to countries that were relatively democratic and had relatively capable states in 2004 and match on region, ethnic fractionalization, time period of democratization, and income at democratization. We then compare the year 2004 values on ln GDP per capita across countries that had relatively high and low scores on the bureaucracy measure *at their first incidence of democratization*. Do these otherwise similar countries differ in income today, *based on their different democratization histories*?[10] The results from Model 5 suggests that they do not.

The five models reported in Table 2 are robust to making various specification changes.[11] The alterations include using the information capacity measure from Brambor et al. (2019) instead of the impartial and rule-following administration measure, V-Dem's Regimes of the World measure instead of median Polyarchy to capture democratization, or Maddison (2007) GDP data instead of the Fariss et al. (2017) data. Further, since the time lag of twenty years between the matching variables and controls, on the one hand, and outcome variable, on the other, is somewhat arbitrary, we repeated the same procedure with various time lags. Results are mostly similar when measuring the dependent variable with different lags – from zero to thirty years – than the benchmark twenty-year lag. Results are somewhat more favorable to a long-term effect in line with the stateness-first argument for countries that undergo democratization when we employ entropy balancing (Hainmueller, 2011) instead of the CEM methodology. Yet, in sum, when performing different analyses on datasets that are pruned to balance covariates and only draw inferences from comparing fairly similar cases – under different assumptions about what constitutes the relevant counterfactuals and comparisons – we identify no consistent pattern that comport with the stateness-first argument.

6.3 Comparing Sequences

Our final approach to testing involves directly comparing the different historical sequences of institutional change that countries have experienced and assessing potential consequences for economic growth. Having differentiated countries according to patterns of institutional change in Section 4, we want to assess whether there are any discernible differences between countries that experienced these different historical patterns. Mainly, we contrast the two sets of countries that are classified with histories comporting to, respectively,

---

[10] This particular specification likely introduces selection bias. By extracting only states that were both fairly democratic and had capable bureaucracies in 2004, we are, for example, selecting democracies that managed to establish strong bureaucracies *in spite* of their problematic historical trajectory (according to the stateness-first argument). This type of selection is not present in the other models in Table 2.

[11] See Section C in the Appendix.

stateness-first and democracy-first sequences. The fundamental implication of the stateness-first argument is that stateness-first patterns, when compared to democracy-first patterns, are positively associated with subsequent economic development. Relative to the panel-tests and the pre-parametric matching analysis, this approach has the benefit of leveraging the entire institutional history of a country (up until a particular point in time) and correlating it with economic growth (in the following years), enabling us to conduct what are arguably more direct assessments of the stateness-first argument's main empirical implication.

To probe the relationship between institutional sequencing histories and economic development, we specify OLS models with country- and year-fixed effects, errors clustered by country and logged GDP p.c. in $t + 20$ as dependent variable. We include dummy variables representing three of the four sequencing types that we discussed in Section 4 (stateness-first is the reference category), including those for which transitions into high-capacity–high-democracy states were not (yet) observed. We note that given the panel nature of the data, a country may count as, for example, right-censored (still not transitioned to a high-high state) early in the time series and either a stateness-first or democracy-first sequence later on. To isolate the effect of the historical *sequencing* of institutional changes from current *levels* of state capacity and democracy (at each point in time), we also include dummy variables representing each of the four states. In some models, we also account for the length of time spent in each state, insofar as we may expect long-term effects of having a long history with a particular historical configuration. This control strategy enables us to isolate variation associated with following a particular sequence from having (a long history of) a particular institutional configuration. Our primary interest is whether countries that had previously transitioned from low democracy–high capacity to high levels of both fared comparatively better or worse than the countries that transitioned from high democracy–low capacity to high levels of both and we therefore focus on the "democracy-first" regression coefficient (we remind that "stateness-first" is the reference category).

In addition to the variables capturing different institutional sequences, Model 1 in Table 3 controls only for initial values of ln GDP p.c., country- and year-fixed effects, and the current institutional state. Model 2 adds four covariates that measure the cumulative number of previous years spent in each of the four institutional states to account for other aspects of a country's institutional history than the sequence of institutional adoption. According to both of these models, future levels of income (i.e., in $t+20$) in countries that followed a democracy-first pattern are not statistically distinguishable from income levels in countries that could be described as stateness-first cases. The point estimates

Table 3 Democracy-first vs. stateness-first sequences and economic development

Cut-off, Polyarchy:	(1) Median b/(se)	(2) Median b/(se)	(3) Median b/(se)	(4) Mean b/(se)	(5) 0.5 b/(se)
Democracy-first	0.009	0.017	0.026	0.079	−0.088
	(0.064)	(0.080)	(0.118)	(0.078)	(0.137)
Right-censored	0.012	0.04	0.211	0.002	−0.178**
	(0.084)	(0.094)	(0.163)	(0.070)	(0.056)
Left-censored	0.185*	0.168	0.224	0.213	0.148
	(0.085)	(0.094)	(0.144)	(0.111)	(0.094)
Low dem., high cap.	0.023	0.035	−0.081	0.019	0.027
	(0.040)	(0.041)	(0.059)	(0.037)	(0.034)
High dem., low cap.	−0.031	−0.017	−0.067*	−0.019	0.038
	(0.034)	(0.033)	(0.033)	(0.036)	(0.049)
High dem., high cap.	0.007	0.018	−0.096	0.027	0.038
	(0.043)	(0.042)	(0.053)	(0.041)	(0.051)
Σ Low dem., low cap.		0.001	0.002	0.001	0.001
		(0.001)	(0.001)	(0.001)	(0.001)
Σ Low dem., high cap.		0	0.001	0.002	0.002
		(0.002)	(0.003)	(0.001)	(0.001)
Σ High dem., low cap.		0.001	0.001	0.005*	0.005
		(0.001)	(0.002)	(0.002)	(0.010)
Σ High dem., high cap.		0.002*	0.002*	0.002*	0.001
		(0.001)	(0.001)	(0.001)	(0.001)
Ln GDP p.c. (LDV)	0.815**	0.791**	0.800**	0.792**	0.803**
	(0.040)	(0.044)	(0.041)	(0.045)	(0.046)
Electoral democracy			−0.071		
			(0.134)		
Impartial public admin.			0.058		
			(0.030)		
Democracy x impartial			−0.029		
			(0.059)		
Civil War			−0.02		
			(0.042)		
Resource dependence			−0.007**		
			(0.002)		
Ln population			0.002		
			(0.043)		
Country fixed effects	Y	Y	Y	Y	Y
Year fixed effects	Y	Y	Y	Y	Y
N	16,080	16,080	10,453	16,080	16,080

Notes: *$p < 0.05$; **$p < 0.01$. OLS with country-year as unit and ln GDP p.c. in $t + 20$ as dependent variable. Errors are clustered by country.

suggest that democracy-first sequences enhance growth, but the *t*-values are close to zero in both specifications. Interestingly, Model 1 suggests that, compared to stateness-first countries, "left-censored" countries that either entered the sample with above-median values of capacity and democracy or that transitioned there from below-median values for both were significantly associated with higher growth. Yet, the result is not robust in Model 2, suggesting that this pattern can be explained, in part, by the length of time that a country spent in the "high capacity–high democracy" state. We highlight that a higher number of years in such a state is positively associated with growth, indicating that institutional history may matter for development (see also Gerring et al., 2005), although not in the particular manner predicted by stateness-first arguments.

Model 3 includes as controls continuous values of democracy and capacity and their interaction (to account for more finely grained differences in current institutions), as well as measures of civil conflict, resource dependence and population size. When employing this extensive control strategy, we fail to find any systematic differences between democracy-first and stateness-first observations in terms of subsequent economic development. Also when we use the mean (rather than median) values on our democracy and state capacity as thresholds for coding observations as high/low (Model 4) or when we use 0.5 as a cut-off on Polyarchy for high democracy (Model 5), the democracy-first and stateness-first sequences remain statistically indifferentiable.

Across models, there is little support for the expectation that countries that underwent stateness-first sequences fared better than those that democratized before achieving high state capacity. For instance, Figure 15 shows "democracy-first" coefficients for different forward-leads on the outcome (ln GDP p.c.), in specifications otherwise similar to Model 2. If anything, any difference between stateness-first and democracy-first countries would appear to favor the latter. At higher leads – implying that we consider associations with longer-term development outcomes – the coefficient on democracy-first transitions is positive and increases slightly. Yet, the uncertainty around the estimate also increases and the difference is never far from zero.

We conducted several other robustness tests on the core sequencing models. The various democracy-first estimates from these tests are summarized in Appendix Figure C.4, which maps the various coefficients (ln GDP p.c. in $t+20$ is the outcome) associated with democracy-first transitions (stateness-first is always the reference category). For instance, we tried using median values of democracy and state capacity *in each year* to differentiate high and low states, thus "historicizing" what we refer to as democratic/undemocratic and high/low capacity, and we also added an interaction between current levels of democracy and state capacity. Further, we tried controlling for ln GDP p.c. at the

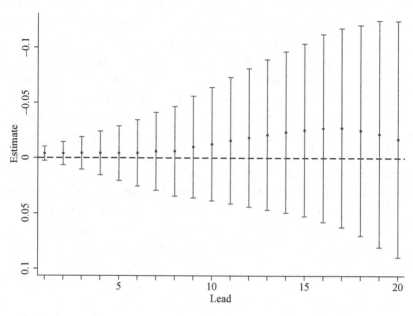

Figure 15 Estimates, with 95% confidence intervals, for democracy-first transitions (relative to stateness-first sequences), for varying time leads on the dependent variable (based on Model 2, Table 3).

time a country first transitioned to high levels of both democracy and state capacity and the average level of ln GDP p.c. before the transition. In other tests, we restricted the sample to countries that had been in a prior state (e.g., high capacity–low democracy) for a minimum of five, ten, and twenty years, as well as for twenty consecutive years, before transitioning to high levels of both democracy and state capacity. We also estimated models using GDP p.c. growth instead of ln GDP p.c. as the dependent variable (both for median and mean thresholds of Polyarchy). Lastly, we estimated models that were similar to Model 2, Table 3, but use the dichotomous BMR democracy measure, and we substituted estimates of impartial public administration with alternative measures of state capacity.

As Appendix Figure C.4 illustrates, the estimated difference between democracy-first and stateness-first countries is positive in some specifications and negative in others. But, the coefficient never reaches conventional thresholds for rejecting the null hypothesis of no difference. We obtain nearly identical results when we use the Maddison instead of Fariss et al. GDP data (see Appendix Figure C.5). In sum, there is considerable evidence that democracy-first countries *did not fare worse* than those that built a relatively strong state before democratizing. Across multiple ways of comparing different patterns of historical institutional changes, the findings (in a few specifications) suggest that, if anything, development outcomes were actually more favorable for democracy-first countries.

7 Conclusion

State building and democratization are salient features of human history, and the historical sequences with which countries have embarked upon these two dual processes of institution building vary considerably. In the premodern period, several historical cases indicate that early democratic institutions – in different regions across the world – seem to have arisen mainly under relatively weak-state conditions, whereas authoritarian systems that achieved strong control over their societies seem to have thrived in polities with strong bureaucracies that could tax and conscript (Stasavage, 2020). Yet other societies seem to have been stuck under conditions of low state capacity and absence of democratic institutions (Acemoglu and Robinson, 2019). In the modern era, after the American and French Revolutions, sequences of state building and democratization have continued to vary substantially. Some countries, such as Greece, started out with weak states before building democracy, while others, such as Denmark, reached relatively high levels of state capacity first, before substantial liberalization of the political regime occurred. In this Element we have focused mainly on sequencing of state building and democratization in the modern era and posed the question: Does such institutional sequences matter for economic development?

More specifically, we have taken a close look at the so-called stateness-first argument, which proposes that the sequence of state building before democratization has benevolent consequences, including for economic development. In addition to presenting this argument and relevant counterarguments, we have criticized current formulations of the argument and tried to clarify it by specifying assumptions and explicitly proposing different, testable empirical implications. By elaborating on the underlying logic of the argument, we have identified and discussed several crucial assumptions about the causal linkages between democracy, state capacity, and growth. We also evaluated the existing empirical evidence base for these assumptions, and find that they do not seem to have strong grounding in existing evidence; sometimes the evidence even indicates that the assumptions are flat-out wrong (at least if they are taken as general propositions). Further, we elaborated on how the stateness-first argument is ambiguous when it comes to specifying the proper counterfactual conditions to a state experiencing the purportedly beneficial stateness-first sequence and what implications this has for empirical testing. By bringing these assumptions and ambiguities into the light, we present a transparent and parsimonious version of the stateness-first argument and a suite of different ways to test (differently specified versions of) the argument empirically.

Our empirical analyses – including case studies of Greece and Denmark as well as a variety of large-N tests on extensive, global samples – suggest that the stateness-first argument has very weak empirical support. Hence, we surmise that the argument may not be valid, at least for explaining general patterns of economic development. We arrive at this conclusion by using new data from V-Dem on countries from across the world, and with time series extending from the year of the French Revolution (1789) to the present, and economic growth or income level as the outcome variable. We test different empirical implications and core assumptions of the stateness-first argument and try out different measures of democracy and state capacity as well as various statistical methods. In most tests, we find no systematic relationships, and only in a few specifications do we find evidence in line with the stateness-first argument. Yet, we should also note that a few other plausible specifications show the exact opposite relationship of what is implied by the stateness-first argument. In sum, we find no convincing evidence that countries became richer because they followed some prescribed "golden sequence" of institutional development. Economic development seems not to be systematically affected by the sequencing of state building and democratization, and can occur both in countries experiencing stateness-first and democracy-first pathways.

The findings presented in this Element point forward toward several avenues for fruitful research. First, one obvious and intriguing extension of this analysis would be to test whether the stateness-first sequence matters differently for other outcomes of relevance, as proposed by existing arguments, such as civil conflict or the survival of democracies. Absent systematic tests, we cannot exclude the possibility that stateness-first transitions have important effects on outcomes other than economic growth. Yet, we caution that our (admittedly very preliminary) analysis on several alternative outcomes in the Appendix (see Section D) do not provide much support for the notions that stateness-first transitions mitigate corruption or clientelism, or mitigate the risk of civil war onset. We find very mixed results on human development as measured by infant mortality rates; some panel regression tests showing clear results in line with the stateness-first argument's key assumption that democracy is more negatively associated with mortality once state capacity increases, but other sequence tests show that stateness-first sequences increase mortality relative to democracy-first sequences. We also find mixed results on long-term democracy levels (for a recent, careful study finding support for certain versions of the stateness-first argument on democratic survival and quality, see Andersen and Doucette, 2020). We believe that these mixed findings warrant more careful studies of stateness-first sequences and alternative outcomes, and we leave more detailed such investigations to future research.

Second, the null-findings presented in this Element might suggest that also other institutionalist explanations that make strong claims about the role of deep institutional histories for economic development (prominent examples being Acemoglu et al., 2001; Evans and Rauch, 1999) – but rely on rough proxy indicators of historical institutions or measuring contemporary institutions and assuming persistence across decades or centuries – should be more closely scrutinized by using refined and direct measures of historical institutions. Third, our discussion of the different counterfactual comparisons required to draw inferences about the effects of stateness-first sequences should inform both theorizing and research designs in future studies of institutional sequencing, so that we ensure that elaborate arguments are tested properly. Fourth, despite the vast amount of attention that has been placed on explaining the institutional determinants of economic development in recent decades, our lack of clear findings suggest that it will be a worthwhile effort to further specify the different mechanisms that generate growth under particular configurations of state-capacity and democracy and study *when* state-capacity and democracy may serve as complements or substitutes in terms of their effects on growth.

The lack of empirical support for the stateness-first argument that is documented in this Element also has ramifications for real-world policy making. Our findings speak to long-standing debates over development policy, state building, and regime change that impact the lives of millions of people across the world. For instance, our findings do not support the widespread notion that foreign development aid needs to be channeled toward building state institutions before, for example, holding multiparty elections, if the ultimate goal is to ensure economic development. The notion that democracy is unsuitable in contexts where weaker state institutions prevail, such as in many countries in contemporary sub-Saharan Africa, Central Asia, or the Middle East, is not uncommon in policy circles. If "bread" is considered a more fundamental goal than "freedom," and democratization is anticipated to come at the cost of a stagnant economy, then foreign ministries, international organizations, and aid agencies may find it preferable to continue to support authoritarian strongmen. Better then, they may consider, to postpone the promotion of democracy until the distant future when state institutions are (hopefully) built and order is ensured. If, however, the trade-off between democratization in low-capacity states and economic development is not as stark, policy makers may rather want to abandon current strongmen and work harder to promote democracy.

Since building state capacity before democratizing is not a requirement for a prospering economy, our findings suggest that democracy advocates in different countries can more wholeheartedly mobilize for democracy also under conditions of weak state institutions. In fact, our results suggest that democracy-first patterns of institutional sequencing may be an equally effective pathway to economic development as the stateness-first pathway. In this regard, our findings could be interpreted as providing some empirical backing for those organizations, opposition movements, and other actors who currently struggle to promote democracy in countries where the state bureaucracy is far from the Weberian ideal. There are more paths to the proverbial "Denmark" than the one historically followed by the actual country of Denmark.

References

Abadie, A., Diamond, A., and Hainmueller, J. (2015). Comparative politics and the synthetic control method. *American Journal of Political Science*, 59(2):495–510.

Acemoglu, D. (2008). *Introduction to Modern Economic Growth*. Princeton University Press, Princeton, NJ.

Acemoglu, D., Johnson, S., and Robinson, J. A. (2001). The colonial origins of comparative development: An empricial investigation. *American Economic Review*, 91(5):1369–1401.

Acemoglu, D., Naidu, S., Restrepo, P., and Robinson, J. A. (2019). Democracy does cause growth. *Journal of Political Economy*, 127(1):47–100.

Acemoglu, D. and Robinson, J. A. (2012). *Why Nations Fail: The Origins of Power, Prosperity and Poverty*. Profile Books, London.

Acemoglu, D. and Robinson, J. A. (2019). *The Narrow Corridor: States, Societies, and the Fate of Liberty*. Penguin Press, New York.

Adsera, A., Boix, C., and Payne, M. (2003). Are you being served? Political accountability and quality of government. *Journal of Law, Economics and Organization*, 19(2):445–490.

Albertus, M. and Menaldo, V. (2012). If you're against them you're with us: The effect of expropriation on autocratic survival. *Comparative Political Studies*, 45(8):973–1003.

Albertus, M. and Menaldo, V. (2018). *Authoritarian and the Elite Origins of Democracy*. Cambridge University Press, Cambridge.

Alesina, A., Devleeschauwer, A., Easterly, W., Kurlat, S., and Wacziarg, R. (2003). Fractionalization. *Journal of Economic Growth*, 8(June):155–194.

Andersen, D. and Cornell, A. (2018). The ambiguous effects of democracy on bureaucratic quality. Working Paper.

Andersen, D. and Doucette, J. (2020). State first? A Disaggregation and empirical interrogation. *British Journal of Political Science*, FirstView.

Andersen, D., Møller, J., Rørbæk, L. L., and Skaaning, S.-E. (2014). State capacity and political regime stability. *Democratization*, 21(7):1305–1325.

Ansell, B. W. and Samuels, D. J. (2014). *Inequality and Democratization*. Cambridge University Press, Cambridge.

Bäck, H. and Hadenius, A. (2008). Democracy and state capacity: Exploring a j-shaped relationship. *Governance*, 21(1):1–24.

Barro, R. J. and Sala-i Martin, X. (2004). *Economic Growth*. The MIT Press, Cambridge, MA.

Benavot, A. and Riddle, P. (1988). The expansion of primary education, 1870–1940: Trends and issues. *American Sociological Association*, 61(3):191–210.

Berman, S. (2007). How democracies emerge: Lessons from Europe. *Journal of Democracy*, 18(1):28–41.

Berman, S. (2019). *Democracy and Dictatorship in Europe: From the Ancien Régime to the Present Day*. Oxford University Press, New York.

Besley, T. and Persson, T. (2009). The origins of state capacity: Property rights, taxation and politics. *American Economic Review*, 99(4):1218–1244.

Besley, T. and Persson, T. (2010). State capacity, conflict and development. *Econometrica*, 78(1):1–34.

Besley, T. and Persson, T. (2011). *Pillars of Prosperity: The Political Economics of Development Clusters*. Princeton University Press, Princeton, NJ.

Bizzarro, F., Gerring, J., Knutsen, C. H., et al. (2018). Party strength and economic growth. *World Politics*, 70(2):275–320.

Blundell, R. and Bond, S. (1998). Initial conditions and moment restrictions in dynamic panel data models. *Journal of Econometrics*, 87(1):115–143.

Bockstette, V., Chanda, A., and Putterman, L. (2002). States and markets: The advantage of an early start. *Journal of Economic Growth*, 7(4):347–369.

Bogaards, M. (2012). Where to draw the line? From degree to dichotomy in measures of democracy. *Democratization*, 19(4):690–712.

Boix, C., Miller, M., and Rosato, S. (2012). A complete data set of political regimes, 1800–2007. *Comparative Political Studies*, 46(12):1523–1554.

Bolt, J. and van Zanden, J. L. (2013). The first update of the Maddison project: Re-estimating growth before 1820. Maddison Project Working Paper 4.

Borcan, O., Olsson, O., and Putterman, L. (2018). State history and economic development: Evidence from six millennia. *Journal of Economic Growth*, 23:1–40.

Brambor, T., Goenaga, A., Lindvall, J., and Teorell, J. (2019). The lay of the land: Information capacity and the modern state. *Comparative Political Studies*, 53(2):175–213.

Brautigam, D., Fjeldstad, O.-H. F., and Moore, M. (2008). *Taxation and State-Building in Developing Countries: Capacity and Consent*. Cambridge University Press, Cambridge.

Bueno de Mesquita, B., Smith, A., Siverson, R. M., and Morrow, J. D. (2003). *The Logic of Political Survival*. MIT Press, Cambridge, MA.

Carbone, G. and Memoli, V. (2015). Does democratization foster state consolidation? Democratic rule, political order, and administrative capacity. *Governance*, 28(1):5–24.

Carothers, T. (2007). The "sequencing" fallacy. *Journal of Democracy*, 18(1):13–27.

Casper, G. and Wilson, M. (2015). Using sequences to model crises. *Political Science Research and Methods*, 3(2):381–397.

Chabal, P. and Daloz, J.-P. (1999). *Africa Works: Disorder as Political Instrument*. James Currey, Oxford.

Charron, N. and Lapuente, V. (2010). Does democracy produce quality of government? *European Journal of Political Research*, 49(4):443–470.

Colagrossi, M., Rossignoli, D., and Maggioni, M. A. (2020). Does democracy cause growth? meta-analysis (of 2000 regressions). *European Journal of Political Economy*, 61(1):Online: 101824.

Coppedge, M., Gerring, J., Altman, D., et al. (2011). Defining and measuring democracy: A new approach. *Perspectives on Politics*, 9(2):247–267.

Coppedge, M., Gerring, J., Glynn, A., et al. (2020a). *Varieties of Democracy: Measuring Two Centuries of Political Change*. Cambridge University Press, Cambridge.

Coppedge, M., Gerring, J., Knutsen, C. H., et al. (2020b). Varieties of democracy (v-dem) dataset v.10. Varieties of Democracy (V-Dem) Project.

Coppedge, M., Gerring, J., Knutsen, C. H., et al. (2020c). Varieties of democracy (v-dem) codebook v.10. Varieties of Democracy (V-Dem) Project.

Cornell, A., Knutsen, C. H., and Teorell, J. (2020). Bureaucracy and growth. *Comparative Political Studies*, 53(14):2246–2282.

Dahl, R. A. (1971). *Polyarchy: Participation and Opposition*. Yale University Press, New Haven, CT.

Dahl, R. A. (1998). *On Democracy*. Yale University Press, New Haven, CT.

D'Arcy, M. and Nistotskaya, M. (2017). State first, then democracy: Using cadastral records to explain governmental performance in public goods provision. *Governance*, 30(2):193–209.

Doucouliagos, H. and Ulubaşoğlu, M. A. (2008). Democracy and economic growth: A meta-analysis. *American Journal of Political Science*, 52(1):61–83.

Esping-Andersen, G. (1990). *The Three Worlds of Welfare Capitalism*. Princeton University Press, Princeton, NJ.

Evans, P. and Rauch, J. E. (1999). Bureaucracy and growth: A cross-national analysis of the effects of "Weberian" state. *American Sociological Review*, 64(5):748–765.

Evans, P. B. (1995). *Embedded Autonomy. States and Industrial Transformation*. Princeton University Press, Princeton, NJ.

Fariss, C. J., Crabtree, C. D., Anders, T., Jones, Z. M., Linder, F. J., and Markowitz, J. N. (2017). Latent estimation of GDP, GDP per capita, and population from historic and contemporary sources. Working Paper.

Fortin-Rittenberger, J. (2014). Exploring the relationship between infrastructural and coercive state capacity. *Democratization*, 21(7):1244–1264.

Fukuyama, F. (2004). *State-Building: Governance and World-Order in the 21st Century*. Cornell University Press, Ithaca, NY.

Fukuyama, F. (2007). Liberalism versus state-building. *Journal of Democracy*, 18(3):10–13.

Fukuyama, F. (2011). Is there a proper sequence in democratic transitions? *Current History*, 110(739):308–310.

Fukuyama, F. (2012). *The Origins of Political Order*. Profile Books, London.

Fukuyama, F. (2014a). *Polticial Order and Political Decay: From the Industrial Revolution to the Globalisation of Democracy*. Profile Books, London.

Fukuyama, F. (2014b). States and democracy. *Democratization*, 21(7):1326–1340.

Galenson, W. (1959). *Labor and Economic Development*. John Wiley and Sons, New York.

Gerring, J., Bond, P., Barndt, W. T., and Moreno, C. (2005). Democracy and economic growth: A historical perspective. *World Politics*, 57(3):323–364.

Gøbel, E. (2003). *De styrede rigerne: Embedsmændene i den dansk-norske centraladministration 1660–1814.* Syddansk Universitetsforlag, Odense.

Haber, S. and Menaldo, V. (2011). Do natural resources fuel authoritarianism? reappraisal of the resource curse. *American Political Science Review*, 105(1):1–26.

Hainmueller, J. (2012). Entropy balancing for causal effects: A multivariate reweighting method to produce balanced samples in observational studies. *Political Analysis*, 20(1):25–46.

Halperin, M. H., Siegle, J. T., and Weinstein, M. M. (2005). *The Democracy Advantage: How Democracies Promote Prosperity and Peace*. Routledge, New York.

Hanson, J. (2015). Democracy and state capacity: Complements or substitutes? *Studies in Comparative International Development*, 50(3):304–330.

Hanson, J. K. and Sigman, R. (2019). Leviathan's latent dimensions: Measuring state capacity for comparative political research. Working Paper.

Harvey, R. A., Hayden, J. D., Kamble, P. S., Bouchard, J. R., and Huang, J. C. (2017). A comparison of entropy balance and probability weighting methods to generalize observational cohorts to a population: a simulation and empirical example. *Pharmacoepidemiology and Drug Safety*, 26:367–377.

Hobson, C. (2012). Liberal democracy and beyond: Extending the sequencing debate. *International Political Science Review*, 33(4):441–454.

Hoeffler, A. E. (2002). The augmented Solow model and the African growth debate. *Oxford Bulletin of Economics and Statistics*, 64(2):135–158.

Honaker, J. and King, G. (2010). What to do about missing values in time-series cross-section data. *American Journal of Political Science*, 54(3):561–581.

Huntington, S. P. (1968). *Political Order in Changing Societies*. Yale University Press, New Haven, CT.

Huntington, S. P. (1991). Democracy's third wave. *Journal of Democracy*, 2(2):12–34.

Iacus, S. M., King, G., and Porro, G. (2012). Causal inference without balance checking: Coarsened exact matching. *Political Analysis*, 20(1):1–24.

Inglehart, R. and Welzel, C. (2005). *Modernization, Cultural Change, and Democracy: The Human Development Sequence*. Cambridge University Press, Cambridge.

Jerven, M. (2013). *Poor Numbers: How We Are Misled by African Development Statistics and What to Do about It*. Cornell University Press, Ithaca, NY.

Kalyvas, S. (2015). *Modern Greece: What Everyone Needs to Know*. Oxford University Press, New York.

Kammas, P. and Sarantides, V. (2020). Democratisation and tax structure in the presence of ome production: Evidence from the Kingdom of Greece. *Journal of Economic Behavior and Organization*, 177:219–236.

Kaufmann, D., Kray, A., and Mastruzzi, M. (2010). The worldwide governance indicators: Methodology and analytical issues. World Bank Policy Research Working Paper 5430.

Kemeny, J. (1995). Theories of power in the three worlds of welfare capitalism. *Journal of European Social Policy*, 5(2):87–96.

Kennedy, R. (2010). The contradiction of modernization: A conditional model of endogenous democratization. *Journal of Politics*, 72(3):785–798.

Knudsen, T. (2006). *Fra Enevælde til Folkestyre. Dansk Demokratihistorie Indtil 1973*. Akademisk Forlag, Copenhagen.

Knutsen, C. H. (2011a). Democracy, dictatorship and protection of property rights. *Journal of Development Studies*, 47(1):164–182.

Knutsen, C. H. (2011b). *The Economic Effects of Democracy and Dictatorship*. PhD thesis, Department of Political Science, University of Oslo.

Knutsen, C. H. (2012). Democracy and economic growth: A survey of arguments and results. *International Area Studies Review*, 15(4):393–415.

Knutsen, C. H. (2013). Democracy, state capacity, and economic growth. *World Development*, 43(March):1–18.

Knutsen, C. H. (2015). Why democracies outgrow autocracies in the long run: Civil liberties, information flows and technological change. *Kyklos*, 68(3):357–384.

Knutsen, C. H., Teorell, J., Wig et al. (2019). Introducing the Historical Varieties of Democracy Dataset: Patterns and Determinants of Democratization in the Long 19th Century. *Journal of Peace Research*, 56(3):440–451.

Lake, D. A. and Baum, M. A. (2001). The invisible hand of democracy: Political control and the provision of public services. *Comparative Political Studies*, 34(6):587–621.

Levi, M. (1989). *Of Rule and Revenue*. University of California Press, Berkeley.

Lindert, P. H. (2005). *Growing Public: Social Spending and Economic Growth since the Eighteenth Century*. Vol. 1. Cambridge University Press, Cambridge.

Lindvall, J. and Teorell, J. (2016). State capacity as power: A conceptual framework. Lund University: STANCE Working Paper No. 1.

Lührmann, A., Tannenberg, M., and Lindberg, S. I. (2018). Regimes of the world (row): Opening new avenues for the comparative study of political regimes. *Politics and Governance*, 6(1):60–77.

Maddison, A. (2007). *Contours of the World Economy 1–2030*. Oxford University Press, Oxford.

Magee, C. S. and Doces, J. A. (2015). Reconsidering regime type and growth: Lies, dictatorships, and statistics. *International Studies Quarterly*, 59(2):223–237.

Mansfield, E. D. and Snyder, J. (1995). Democratization and the danger of war. *International Security*, 20(1):5–38.

Mansfield, E. D. and Snyder, J. (2005). *Electing to Fight: Why Emerging Democracies Go to War*. MIT Press, Cambridge, MA.

Mansfield, E. D. and Snyder, J. L. (2007). The sequencing "fallacy." *Journal of Democracy*, 18(3):5–10.

Marshall, M. G. and Jaggers, K. (2007). Polity IV Project: Dataset Users' Manual.

Marshall, T. H. (1949). *Citizenship and Social Class*. Pluto, London.

Mazzuca, S. and Munck, G. L. (2014). State or democracy first? Alternative perspectives on the state-democracy nexus. *Democratization*, 21(7):1221–1243.

Migdal, J. S. (1988). *Strong Societies and Weak States: State-Society Relations and State Capabilities in the Third World*. Princeton University Press, Princeton, NJ.

Miller, M. K. (2015). Democratic pieces: Autocratic elections and democratic development since 1815. *British Journal of Political Science*, 45(3):501–530.

Møller, J. (2015). The medieval roots of democracy. *Journal of Democracy*, 26(3):110–123.

Møller, J. and Skaaning, S.-E. (2013). Regime types and democratic sequencing. *Journal of Democracy*, 24(1):142–155.

Mudge, S. L. and Chen, A. S. (2014). Political parties and the sociological imagination: Past, present, and future directions. *Annual Review of Sociology*, 40:305–330.

North, D. C. (1990). *Institutions, Institutional Change and Economic Performance*. Cambridge University Press, Cambridge.

North, D. C. (2005). *Understanding the Process of Economic Change*. Princeton University Press, Princeton, NJ.

Olson, M. (1982). *The Rise and Decline of Nations. Economic Growth, Stagflation and Social Rigidities*. Yale University Press, New Haven, CT.

Olson, M. (1993). Dictatorship, democracy, and development. *American Political Science Review*, 87(3):567–576.

Papaioannou, E. and Siourounis, G. (2008). Democratization and growth. *Economic Journal*, 118(532):1520–1551.

Przeworski, A. (1991). *Democracy and the Market: Political and Economic Reforms in Eastern Europe and Latin America*. Cambridge University Press, Cambridge.

Przeworski, A., Alvarez, M. E., Cheibub, J. A., and Limongi, F. (2000). *Democracy and Development. Political Institutions and Well-Being in the World, 1950–1990*. Cambridge University Press, Cambridge.

Przeworski, A. and Limongi, F. (1993). Political regimes and economic growth. *Journal of Economic Perspectives*, 7(3):51–69.

Przeworski, A. and Limongi, F. (1997). Modernization: Theories and Facts. *World Politics*, 49(2):155–183.

Robinson, J. A. and Verdier, T. (2013). The political economy of Clientelism. *Scandinavian Journal of Economics*, 115(2):260–291.

Rodrik, D. (1991). Policy uncertainty and private investment in developing countries. *Journal of Development Economics*, 36(2):229–242.

Rodrik, D., Subramanian, A., and Trebbi, F. (2004). Institutions rule: The primacy of institutions over geography and integration in economic development. *Journal of Economic Growth*, 9(2):131–165.

Romer, P. (1990). Endogenous technological change. *Journal of Political Economy*, 98(5):71–102.

Rustow, D. A. (1970). Transitions to democracy: Toward a dynamic model. *Comparative Politics*, 2(3):337–363.

Schweinitz Jr., K. d. (1959). Industrialization, labor controls, and democracy. *Economic Development and Cultural Change*, 7(4):385–404.

Scott, J. (1998). *Seeing Like a State*. Yale University Press, New Haven, CT.

Seeberg, M. B. (2015). *The Contingent Effect of Authoritarian Elections*. PhD thesis, Aarhus University.

Sen, A. (1999). *Development as Freedom*. Anchor Books, New York.

Shefter, M. (1993). *Political Parties and the State*. Princeton University Press, Princeton, NJ.

Stasavage, D. (2005). Democracy and educational spending in Africa. *American Journal of Political Science*, 49(2):343–358.

Stasavage, D. (2020). *The Decline and Rise of Democracy: A Global History from Antiquity to Today*. Princeton University Press, Princeton, NJ.

Teorell, J., Coppedge, M., Lindberg, S., and Skaaning, S.-E. (2019). Measuring polyarchy across the globe, 1900–2017. *Studies in Comparative International Development*, 54(1):71–95.

Tilly, C. (1990). *Coercion, Capital and European States, A.D. 990–1992*. Cambridge: Wiley-Blackwell.

van Ham, C. and Seim, B. (2017). Strong states, weak elections? How state capacity in authoritarian regimes conditions the democratizing power of elections. *International Political Science Review*, 39(1):49–66.

Wang, E. H. and Xu, Y. (2018). Awakening Leviathan: The effect of democracy on state capacity. *Research & Politics*, 5(2):2053168018772398.

Weber, M. ([1918]1968). *Economy and Society*. University of Carlifornia Press, Berkeley.

Zakaria, F. (2003). *The Future of Freedom. Illiberal Democracy Home and Abroad*. W. W. Norton, New York.

Ziblatt, D. (2017). *Conservative Parties and the Birth of Modern Democracy in Europe*. Cambridge: Cambridge University Press.

Cambridge Elements ≡

Political Economy

David Stasavage
New York University

David Stasavage is Julius Silver Professor in the Wilf Family Department of Politics at New York University. He previously held positions at the London School of Economics and at Oxford University. His work has spanned a number of different fields and currently focuses on two areas: development of state institutions over the long run and the politics of inequality. He is a member of the American Academy of Arts and Sciences.

About the Series

The Element Series Political Economy provides authoritative contributions on important topics in the rapidly growing field of political economy. Elements are designed so as to provide broad and in-depth coverage combined with original insights from scholars in political science, economics, and economic history. Contributions are welcome on any topic within this field.

Cambridge Elements ≡

Political Economy

Elements in the Series

A full series listing is available at: www.cambridge.org/EPEC

Printed in the United States
by Baker & Taylor Publisher Services